ONE YEAR IN WONDE
A True Tale of Expat Life
By Christopher R. Cor

Based on the blog *"Beer and Bloating in Dubai"*

© 2011 Christopher Combe. All rights reserved.
ISBN 978-1-4709-5267-9

To my wife and children, who indulge my daydreams but keep my feet on the ground.

The end and the beginning

I leave Dubai almost exactly one year on from when I was offered the chance to go there. I received the offer via telephone while on holiday with my family in South Wales. The sun shone in a cloud-free Permbrokeshire sky for almost the whole week of our stay, giving me a taste – just a taste – of what to expect from the weather in the Arabian Gulf. Surely you can never tire of blue skies, can you?

And now, a full year later, and with a head full of conflicting regrets and gut-knotting trepidation, I set off on my final drive to the airport, taking the chance to have one last look at the iconic buildings and developments stretching along the length of the Jumeirah Beach Road. As I drive, cheesy MOR rock music plays on the radio, and I actually feel a small but significant pang of regret about leaving Dubai. Maybe I am emotional because my wife and kids left over a month ago, and maybe I feel that I've messed everything up and let everyone down, but there is the ghost of a lump in my throat as I mentally wave goodbye to the magnificent, sprawling Madinat Jumeirah, the brilliant-white, sail-shaped Burj Al Arab and the sea-blue, wave-like structure of the Jumeirah Beach Hotel.

As I continue my final drive along the beach road, I feel a slight temptation to turn off towards the public beach near the Burj and watch one more Gulf sunset over Jumeirah beach, but decide against it. Time is moving on, and I have a plane to catch, so I head back onto the main highway, and I am soon gliding along between the glittering skyscrapers that stand guard on either side of the Sheik Zayed Road. A few minutes later I pass over the unusually traffic-free Garhoud Bridge and on towards the airport.

Before I know it, the hire car has been deposited and I am checked in, waiting in the departure gate for the call to board. I sit quietly, thinking about the past and the future, wondering if I was doing the right thing. In the end, I am glad to get on the plane and take off into yet another cloudless, blue sky. From my window seat I watch the land receding rapidly beneath me, and as we head over the long, straight, golden-edged coast and over the Arabian Gulf, I look down on the man-made islands in the shape of the world and a palm tree, and spot the distinctive shapes of the two hotels I had passed just a few hours earlier. When they disappear from view behind me, I turn away and find myself thinking:

Who dreams this stuff up?

And so the decision has been made, and on reflection I think it was the right one. Dubai drove me to distraction and messed with my head. It had countless, glorious sunny days, quiet beaches with warm cobalt water and golden sand, and the finest food and beverages were always close to hand. It also had too many obscenely hot days, when stepping outside was for mad dogs and masochists; it had sand and dust storms that didn't relent for days and traffic that snarled and honked all around you. Last, but certainly not least, it had a glaring, appalling inequality that - when you eventually chose to take the designer sunglasses off and *really* see it – hit you square in the face like the sudden reflection of the Arabian sun in a high-rise window.

It had been what many would call "an experience".

It was by no means a complete waste of time; money, perhaps, but not time. I learned a great deal about the world, myself, and my family. I had a peek into a shallow world of pampered expatriate existence, but also found honest, unfortunate people who had paid for a dream but had unwrapped a nightmare.

I also gained an insight into the startling phoenix-like rise of Dubai and the United Arab Emirates, and I witnessed first hand what happens when a culture completely changes in the space of thirty or forty years.

People talk about cultural erosion in Britain, but for me it is nothing compared to what has happened - and is happening – in Dubai and, to a lesser extent, the rest of the GCC region. When I was born in1970 the world was certainly a different place, and up until the discovery of oil in the last few years of the 1960s, the UAE was in a different universe. Dubai had been a small pearling and trading outpost, with a transient, nomadic population concentrated around the creek. Mains electricity and water were only introduced in the 1950s, and in the same decade the British built the first airport, which was essentially a shed in a nice, flat piece of desert.

The oil changed everything. Immigrant labour flooded in from the nearby sub-continental countries, tripling the population in the space of seven years. The early 1970s saw the independence from British colonial protection and unification of the seven emirates into the United Arab Emirates and growth continued through the decade, assisted by the influx of large numbers of Lebanese immigrants bent on escape from civil war. In 1979, Jebel Ali Free Port was opened, featuring the largest man-made harbour in the world, attracting even more immigrant labour and trade from around the world. Through the '90s, many international businesses shifted their concerns to Dubai, which was perceived as a more stable, safer location than the likes of Kuwait and Bahrain in the aftermath of the first Gulf War.

The arrival of the new millennium brought new challenges for the rulers of the emirate. Oil reserves were starting to dwindle when global oil prices were increasing. The focus shifted towards tourism, and high-end hotels and resorts began to emerge up from the sand. The growth exploded. An uncle of mine, reminiscing about his days in the Royal Navy on a minesweeper in the Persian Gulf in the early '90s, told me that his ship often docked in Jebel Ali to refuel and the sailors would drive the half-hour to Dubai for beer and entertainment.

In the year 2000 Dubai and Jebel Ali were separate towns. Almost marking the halfway point between them, beside the Sheik Zayed Road, there stood a sand-blown outpost called the Hard Rock Café.

By the time I arrived in 2006, the mock skyscraper of the Hard Rock Café was surrounded by the fifty-storey towers of the sprawling new development that is Dubai Marina. The Sheik Zayed Road - now an eight-lane highway acting as the spine of Dubai - was lined with residential and industrial areas and titanic shopping malls and Jebel Ali had become just another suburb of Dubai.

What is difficult to appreciate without being there is that it's nowhere near finished. I have never seen so many cranes in one place in my life, and I doubt I will again. Some days, the dust thrown up by construction activities mingles with sandstorms to create an impenetrable milky gloom. Mammoth roadside billboards herald the imminent commencement or completion of yet another gigantic development, invariably named Falcon City or Sports City or Some Other Bloody City, covering the desert with yet more concrete, steel, tarmac and luscious, green, constantly-watered grass.

Not that I'm complaining, of course. The very reason I came to Dubai was to work in the construction industry. As it was, I didn't even work on that many jobs in Dubai itself. Such is the knock-on effect of the property and business boom around the region that the bulk of my time was spent working on a project in Doha, Qatar being built by a Dubai developer. At least I got to see other cities in the region, which was useful for comparison purposes, in hindsight.

It's not really a surprise, then, that the place has become what it is today: a seething, multicultural, multi-*class*, melting-pot metropolis favoured by footballers and low-rent celebrities. It's also not really a surprise that the unfettered, exponential growth has started to cause major problems due to inadequate, tagged-on infrastructure and rising costs of living for the people living and working there. What *is* a surprise is that the place has so far held together pretty well with all the changes it has seen and the number of foreigners that have moved here.

One has to realize that this country and this city rose from the desert sands in only a few decades and, when you scrape away the wafer-thin veneer that the marketing people show to the outside world, you can see that it is still only a very young country with rules and laws that are being refined or even just created. Some people may get the impression that the rulers are trapped in the Dark Ages, when it seems evident that they are just trying their best to maintain cultural and religious traditions whilst looking to embrace the modernization and tolerance that they know is necessary for success in the modern global economy.

What follows is the story of my family's time in Dubai, but it tells more than just a tale of life in the Arabian Gulf.

AUGUST

Saturday, August 26, 2006

I'm New Around Here.

So please be gentle, Dubai.

Well actually, I've been in Dubai for nearly three weeks now. It's frightening how quickly it has flown, but in a peculiar way it also feels like I've been here for months and months. This is probably because so much has happened in such a short time. Six weeks ago – maybe even less time than that - this was nothing more than a crazy idea, and now I'm here.

When I stepped off the KLM flight from Amsterdam at around 10pm on 5th August, I thought to myself, "where's this heat everyone warned me about?" That would come later, because I was still in a nice, air-conditioned environment. But, by gosh and golly, what a big airport it is; or so it seemed, because it took so long to taxi to the gate after landing. The walk through the airport was good for stretching the old legs after the six hour flight, and I was able to have a good gawp at my new surroundings and the huge variety of people coming and going.

Despite it being one of the busiest times of the week, passport control wasn't too bad, other than having some rude American fellow jumping the queue just in front of me and mumbling some excuse that I was too tired to argue with. After collecting my bags I finally stepped out into the open air to look for my hotel pick-up and the heat hit me like the blast from a just-opened oven door. It really was astonishing, even at this hour. I found the man holding the placard bearing my name and was escorted through muggy air - which I drank as much as breathed - to a mini-bus that was my ride to the hotel. It was a short journey that I don't remember much about; I was absolutely shattered.

I got to the hotel, checked in, and got taken to my room. I instantly decided it was crap. The sign outside tried to give the impression that it was not just a hotel, but luxury hotel apartments. Well, that was bollocks, quite frankly. Fully-equipped kitchen, my hat. Since when did a surface-top hotplate, a fridge and a washing machine made in Communist-era Eastern Europe constitute fully-equipped? Some rusty cutlery and chipped crockery completed the paltry ensemble. At least there was a clean bed there to sleep on and a TV to watch.

Sleep? That's a laugh. Obviously the time difference caused a few days' worth of minor sleep problems, but that's nothing. I suppose part of this whole multi-cultural exposure deal when you come to a new country is getting used to the strange habits of other cultures. It was as if the place came alive at 11.30pm, a time when I am usually trying to get off into the land of nod. Doors slamming, kids running around, people shouting along the corridors.....WILL YOU SHUT UP?! Don't these people sleep?

I remember being woken the first morning by the sound of the dawn call to prayer, a sound I had heard on TV and movies, but which was an altogether different experience in the "flesh". The amplified singing from the many mosques in the area echoed around the streets with an eerie, haunting quality that was actually quite soothing. I managed to get back to sleep for another hour or so before seeking out breakfast, but shouldn't have bothered: it was mostly lukewarm slop and not a scrap of real bacon or a sausage was to be found. I went for the safe toast and jam option.

On my first full day in Dubai it appeared that I had to make my own way to work. I had received no contact from my new Employers, and no offers to send someone along to meet me, so I showed some initiative and rang them after breakfast to find out if I was in the right city at the right time. I was, thank goodness, and received instructions on how to get to the office. There was no address as we are accustomed to in the UK, just a building name (Something something office), the name of the area (Oud Metha) and a few landmarks (Wafi City / Citibank Tower). I wrote it down to tell the taxi driver and got a hotel chap to flag a cab down for me.

I had to wait a while and, like a fool, stood there in the already-baking morning heat, suited and booted for that all-important first day, sweating like the proverbial, bacon-producing, forbidden creature and squinting hard against the glare from the sky and the light-coloured buildings all around. I had left my prescription sunglasses back in the UK. Good start, eh? (I would never see through those sunglasses again. My wife dutifully posted them in a little package to my work PO Box address, but the package never arrived. You soon learn to make other arrangements for sending and receiving anything of value in the UAE)

My first day wasn't too stressful. The office manager was out at meetings all day, so I sat in an office with one of my new colleagues – a young British go-getter who was obviously working his way up the corporate ladder – and listened to his mixture of advice, urban legends and glowing self admiration.

I spent a couple of days using taxis to get back and forth to the office, but it wasn't long before the lovely admin people there arranged a hire car for me. It was something like a Honda Civic, in the obligatory dusty white, but it looked like a beaten-up old dodgem with little dents and scratches all over it. Obviously, it didn't have a pole for the electric feed at the back, and it didn't have a thick rubber bumper all the way round, but to be honest, they should make all the cars here like that. It would be much more fun.

My first experience of the infamous Sheik Zayed Road was pretty much like a ten-lane version of said dodgems, only without the tattooed men clambering all over the vehicles. Monstrous, black-windowed 4x4s screamed past on all sides, mini-buses tailgated me, and Pakistani men on bicycles pedalled towards me on the wrong side of the road. It's a struggle to remain calm in these conditions, and the temptation to give rude hand signals to the inevitable headlight-flashing tail-gaters has to be resisted. I've already heard one or two tales from my new colleagues of people getting into trouble for giving the middle finger to Arab drivers. It's a strict no-no in this part of the world, or you can expect to be on the plane home very swiftly indeed.

When I get the chance to get out of the car and enter any public space (making sure I park as close to the building as possible), such as a mall, I am confronted with a bewildering variety of races and cultures...and that's just the shops. I'm not whingeing here. This is all part of life's rich tapestry and is something I will remember for the rest of my days. The melting pot feel of the place is really something. It's like being in the Star Wars Cantina in Mos Eisley, although I haven't yet met anyone who has the death sentence in twelve systems.

Then there's the main reason I actually came here, which you can't fail to miss with all the cranes on the skyline. The building work going on is amazing in scale and in scope, even if there is a slight nagging doubt at the back of my mind, mainly to do with that biblical parable about the man who built his house on the sand.

I've had a good old explore already and want to see more when it gets cooler, having been confined to the inside of houses, offices, shopping malls and hotels up until now. I'd definitely like to see more of the authentic Arab culture, which seems to be a bit lacking, or just hard to find, in Dubai itself. I've got myself a local mobile phone SIM card which works on a pay-as-you go card system called Wasl. The cards can be bought almost everywhere, and local calls seem cheap enough.

Thanks to the internet and expat messageboards, I've met a few fellow expat people outside of work, which is just as well because my work colleagues haven't really shown any sort of inclination towards socialising yet. It could be just me, of course, and they could be going out to party wildly every night and not inviting me. Such is the way my paranoid mind works, I'm afraid to say. But like I say, I've met other people and have visited one or two bars so far, including inadvertent visits (thanks to mischievous new friends) to some innocent-enough-sounding but decidedly seedy venues full of Chinese ladies offering "massages", which surprised me given the preconceptions one can gain about life in a Muslim country. I really didn't expect prostitution to be so out in the open and unhidden. I didn't expect it to exist here at all, but maybe I'm just being naive.

I'm hoping there's more to life here than just shopping, drinking and fighting off Chinese ladies of the night and maybe one day I'll be able to steer some unfortunate sod towards the York Hotel or Thank God It's Thursday. Of course, he may feel fortunate, depending on his outlook on life...

Now I just have to furnish the villa that I found ready for the arrival of my family on 3rd September. That is going to mean a visit to the whole forced-route, weird name hell that is IKEA. I hope the wife and kids like the new gaff. It's located in a development called Springs, which is part of a larger area called Emirates Hills (home of the golf course where they hold the Dubai Desert Classic, don't you know?), just off the Sheik Zayed Road, almost opposite the Marina. The houses are a bit uniform and boxy, and the streets are like mazes, but the villa I've found is more than big enough for our needs, and has a pleasantly light and airy feel to it, with white walls, tiled floors and large, screen-festooned windows. It has a decent-sized garden as well, which I will need to get some grass on at some point...at the moment it's just an over-sized sand-pit. Well, you could say that about the whole city, if you were being cynical.

Luckily for me my company are lending me the year's rental money and letting me pay it back monthly rather than leaving me to find just shy of twenty thousand quid to pay all the rent up-front, as is the custom here. If you're blessed you may be allowed to pay it in two instalments, but that invariably adds a few more thousand to the annual rent. It cost me a tad more than I had been expecting, but it seemed to be the going rate for a villa of this size. I looked in other areas such as Mirdiff (too many low-flying planes on final approach into DXB), but this area seemed best, and the Real Estate agent assigned to me by the HR lady at work seemed straight enough, unlike another agent who showed me a property I'd already seen the previous day but who said the rent was ten grand more.

My commute to work won't be too bad, as I will be heading the opposite way to the bulk of the traffic that comes across the creek from Deira and Sharjah. There's also a good British school near the villa as well, and I hope to get my son into it. I can't wait to get out of this excuse, either, particularly as they've started doing renovation works to the reception area.

So, let's get it on. We've got a long journey ahead of us, and I can't wait for the family to arrive and join in with the experience.

SEPTEMBER

Tuesday, September 05, 2006

They're Here!

No, not the Magic Camels of Nad Al Sheba, or the Mystical Maniacs of Sheik Zayed Road - no, my wife and kiddies! Woo-hoo!

I tell you what, though, what a bloody going on it was getting them into the country. It took almost two hours for them to get from the plane to the meet-and-greet area just outside the airport doors. With our mobile phones not wanting to work for one reason or another, we were unable to communicate, so I must have turned about four different shades of red while I was stood waiting for them, and it wasn't because of the heat. In the end, we almost bumped into each other by accident. I was starting to get really agitated, so stomped into the airport building to ask every official-looking Tom, Dick and Mohammed where they could be, before storming outside again and catching a glimpse of my anxious and tired-looking wife standing around wondering where the hell I was (if not where the hell she was). She was glad to see me, if only so I could take an over-tired, clingy child and a couple of heavy bags away from her.

Anyway, they're here now, and it's like a whole other chapter of our lives has begun. The chapter involving my time alone and scared in this crazy city is over, and now the chapter with my family begins. I hope they like it, and so far they seem to be getting into it. My six-year-old son, Joseph, is taking to his new school like a duck to hoi sin sauce. I managed to get him into the Dubai British School in Springs quite easily in the end, in spite of the horror stories about finding a place that I have read. Emma, my sweet little two-year-old daughter, had a little bit of an unsettled first night in her rather bare and echo-prone new bedroom, but now she couldn't seem to care less as long as she gets her dose of kids TV and regular food. Teresa, my wife of 11 years, is just bamboozled, trying to learn how to drive an automatic on the wrong side of the car and the wrong side of the bloody road, surrounded by apparently fearless folk in fast-moving Land Cruisers.

They seem fairly happy with the villa I found for us as well, even if it's a little sparse at the moment. I'm sure we will have to endure more trips to IKEA to find some soft furnishings and pictures for the walls and make the place more homely. We also need some soft play mats for the hard tiled floor. Joseph already has a large bump on his head as the result of an inadvertent head/floor interface situation, otherwise known as six-year-olds charging around without a care in the world, as is their wont.

And then work kicked off big style. It would do, this week, wouldn't it? I've kind of been sitting on the sidelines up until now, like a spectator watching a really fast and scary ride at the fairground, such as the waltzer. Now I've suddenly been pushed onto the ride and getting spun around as fast as possible by the biggest, hairiest, tattoo-adorned fairground worker you've ever seen. Wa-hey! This is fun!

You see, the jobs over here are just immense. All these piddly little buildings back in the UK I used to work on are just small fry, like the kiddies' rollercoaster shaped like a caterpillar with a drugs habit. This work is like the Oblivion and the Nemesis at Alton Towers rolled into one, followed by a kick in the bollocks by Roy Keane for good measure. You stop to look at the figures on the page, and realise that you're shuffling around hundreds of millions of pounds. It's best not to think about it too much, really.

So, onwards and upwards we go. I just hope to the heavens above that my health holds out here. My heart arrhythmia has had a couple of moments so far, but I think I know how to control it. The downside is that I can't drink too much, if you can call that a downside. The upside is it will save me money. But then again, I'll probably just eat more to compensate. We're going for our first Friday brunch tomorrow, where we get to eat and drink as much as we like for about twenty quid! Yippee!

Thursday, September 07, 2006

Fairground Attraction

Yes, I realise that I've made two entries and that both contain fairground analogies. You know why though, don't you? It's because this place really is like Disneyland for adults.

Sunday, September 10, 2006

It Was Like Watching A Car Crash

Except, I missed the actual crash. On the way home tonight, I saw the aftermath of yet another accident on the roads of Dubai. As I drove by I spotted an ambulance and a couple of cars - one of which was on its roof - just off a roundabout on the Al Khail Road (which is supposedly safer and slower than the Sheik Zayed Road). Cars were slowing right down for a good ghoulish gawp, and there were no police anywhere to be seen. No lanes were closed off at all. It was the same with a lorry that had over-turned, which I saw the other day, again on a roundabout on the AK road. No wonder people drive like they do here. You hardly see any police on the road, so the chances of enforcing the rules (which aren't that great, it is not actually illegal to tailgate here, I am lead to believe) are both slim and fat at the same time. The driving here would make even Michael Schumacher cringe, I'm sure.

I found myself actually looking forward to going to work today. Crazy behaviour, I know. I must seek help, and soon. Still, the particular job I'm working on is a huge one in Doha, Qatar, but it's made more interesting by the fact that the project has gone totally and utterly nipples-north. The meetings don't send me to sleep for a change, they actually grab my attention. It helps that there are about ten different nationalities around the table. I really have to pay attention to what people are saying with all the different accents being used, and sit in total awe as a Scotsman talks to a Yemeni, and then a Frenchman interjects, before a Liverpudlian starts waving his arms around and telling everyone to simmer down. I admit I came here with something of a preconception about the Arabs and the way they do business, but the ones I've dealt with so far are cool customers, who don't mind having a bit of banter with you. I thought they'd be aloof and business-like to a T. My only gripe is with them is their habit of breaking into Arabic without warning. If you have a paranoid mind like mine, you imagine them talking about you.

"Did you hear what that fat English dick-head just said?"

"Yeah, what an idiot! I can't believe we're paying hundreds of dirhams an hour for these camel-fancying numpties!"

Ah, such is life. The weather will get better shortly, or so we have been told, and we can get out of the buildings and get some fresh dust...I mean air. This morning, I woke to an extraordinary and alarming sight: overcast skies and fog in Dubai. I thought I'd dreamt the last five weeks and was back in bad old blighty. For a moment I considered ringing Sheik Mo and asking him what the bloody hell was going on. Oy, Mo! Where's the sun, me old mucker? I decided against it in the end (I didn't have his number to hand) and I drove to work in a misty, sunless void, surrounded by petrified locals who drove marginally slower than usual and confused Indians pootling along in the fog, noses pressed against the windscreen of their Nissan Sunnys and hazard lights flashing.

What's that all about? It's not the first time I've seen this, either. If anything out of the ordinary happens, the hazards go on. And when the hazards go on, the driver is suddenly exempt from all rules of the road, and becomes invisible and immune to all external influences. This is especially the case when they double park and block everyone else behind them. I'm not really here! I can do anything I want!

And so, we've come full circle, at full speed around this roundabout to driving in the UAE. It's like a fairground, I tell thee!

Monday, September 11, 2006
Fog On The Creek is all Mine, all Mine

There was an even thicker fog on the way to work this morning, which meant more people with hazard lights blinking stupidly, and police everywhere for a change - not that they were doing anything worthwhile - all they were doing was directing (i.e. blocking) traffic on the roundabout near Springs where the Emirates Road meets Al Khail Road. Complete and utter madness.

Work was good again today. There were more meetings about massive amounts of money and some really first-rate, heated discussions, which are always fun to watch if you can avoid getting dragged into them. As the new boy, I am still able to plead a certain amount of ignorance. The weirdest bit about today was arriving at the meeting just as a few of the local guys were discussing the events of exactly five years ago, namely the 9/11 terrorist attacks in the USA. There were some interesting and quite outlandish theories being bandied about, and extreme differences of opinion on who or what was responsible and who or what was controlling those planes. It reminded me of when I worked on a project in Northern Ireland and was in a meeting where it quickly became obvious that old scars run deep. When the issue of site security came up, the local participants took turns at blaming respective paramilitary groups for various problems in the community. Fortunately no-one got kneecapped on that occasion, and like today, I decided to keep my mouth tightly shut and listen with interest.

But, talking of work and (gulp) flying, I'm off to Doha on Wednesday. It should be interesting to see another bit of the Middle East, and possibly somewhere a bit more "real" than Dubai.

Tuesday, September 12, 2006
The Day Of The Camel

I finally saw my first live camels today on the way to work. As I emerged from a dense bank of fog near the Nad Al Sheba racetrack I had to slow down for the aftermath of yet another car crash. It was then that I caught sight of about 20 of these unique, magnificent yet ungainly beasts trotting along the racetrack to my right, heading for their morning training. One or two had a little black, Dusty Bin-shaped object sitting on top of them just behind the hump. I guessed these were some kind of remote-control jockey.

I wasn't the only one to spot a camel or two. The good lady wife strapped Emma into her hire car and went for a little drive today. She's getting brave now, and decided to venture outside of the relative safety of the Emirates Hills development, and headed to the Ibn Battuta Shopping Mall, which is named after a famous Arabian traveller (how apt). The mall is themed around the various places he visited, with a Chinese court and an Indian court and so on. It is quite an interesting mall, as malls go, and has some educational displays to look at, as well as a full-size replica of a Chinese junk. It's also a lot quieter than the Mall of the Emirates, but is all on ground level, and stretches for over a kilometre from end to end.

Anyway, I digress. Teresa managed to miss her turning from the Sheik Zayed Road, which I will admit is an easy thing to do, and she ended up driving in the general direction of Abu Dhabi with a rising sense of panic. She phoned me from a petrol station, jabbering on about being in the middle of the desert and having nearly collided with a group of camels (I wonder what the collective term is). With the help of a few calming words ("Calm down, you silly moo," didn't work initially), she got the message that she had to turn off the main road ASAP and double back for Dubai. She managed to do that, get to the mall for some retail therapy and a calming cup of coffee, and get home in one piece.

As I told her later, it's all part of the experience of this place. The roads and signs are confusing and misleading and in no time at all you can end up more lost than a group of sickeningly photogenic people who have crashed on a mysterious tropical island. You can usually see the place you want to get to from the main road, but actually getting to it can be a real challenge unless you know the precise place names to look for and which and slip-road to take. Direct left turns are almost completely impossible, with the roads following some weird American-influenced layout us Brits struggle to fathom. Give the Magic Roundabout in Swindon any day. Thank the Lord the signs have English writing as well as Arabic on them, or we'd really be buggered.

I got lost every day for my first week, which was infuriating, but in the longer term this actually helped me because I got to know the names of places quite quickly, building up my mental map and filling in the gaps. I'm now fairly comfortable with getting around, although it is still possible to take the wrong turning and end up in some dusty industrial estate or find oneself heading out into the desert towards Saudi Arabia.

Later today I heard a bit of bad news about a friend I made early on during my time here. This chap had taken me under his wing, invited me for a beer, and had sent me to some of the more "interesting" places in Dubai for a laugh. He had also been good enough to rent the spare room in his lovely, huge villa in Jumeirah (I think it's probably Al Safa really, but we keep that quiet for some reason) to me for a couple of weeks so I could get out of the crappy London Crown Hotel Apartments while I was waiting for Teresa and the kids to come to Dubai

Anyway, apart from one short e-mail, I hadn't heard from him since I had moved into our villa a couple of weeks ago, and so today at lunch I sent a text message to a mate of his asking after him. The ominous message, "Call me," came back. Oh, bugger. The worst of worst things went through my mind, and when I rang up I found out that he had been dune-bashing in his Jeep last weekend and had somehow managed to somersault the bloody thing over a dune and had broken his neck in five places. I wasn't sure how that was exactly possible, but he told me it had been touch-and-go as to whether he would be paralysed or not. It seems he has been quite lucky and has just(!) cracked the vertebrae in his neck, without damaging the spinal cord.

Apparently he is now resting up at home in a neck brace. No doubt he has a little bell by his side which he uses to summon the servants.

Friday, September 15, 2006

Drunk and Dirty In Doha

Please excuse the excitable tone, but I have now seen another place in the Middle East. On Wednesday I took the 7am flight from DXB to Doha, Qatar, for a meeting about the main project I work on, which I will refer to as the Big Hole in the Ground from now on. It is supposed to turn become the Tallest Building in Doha, eventually.

I was, as ever, over-cautious and boy-scoutish in my preparation, and struggled out of bed at 4.15am to get to the airport. I arrived just after 5am – two hours before check-in as advised – and had a long, sleepy wait for the plane, taking in the delights of the crowded departure lounges (even at that time) and the crappy service at Costa (bombfora) Coffee. The flight itself was only forty-five minutes, about the same as Durham Tees Valley to Heathrow, if not shorter. Barely enough time to get nervous, but I still managed it. Flying and me just don't see eye-to-eye.

I arrived in Doha at 7am, Qatar time. The passport control involved some brusque questioning about the nature of my visit and having to pay fifty-five Qatari Riyals by credit card for the visitor's visa. With time to kill in the tiny space that is Doha International Airport, Costa bleeding packet was my only option, so I had another coffee and sat there wondering what day it was, what my name was and why birds suddenly appear every time you are near.

Eventually I left the airport and got in a taxi to take me to the site office, which the taxi driver seemed unable to locate despite the twenty-foot-high hoardings bearing the name of the project placed alongside the road we were driving along. On the way, I took in the delights of Doha, Qatar. It is much more Middle Eastern that Dubai (which isn't hard from what I've seen so far, frankly). The first thing you notice is that there is more space and more greenery, and the long, arcing road that forms the Corniche around the bay is really quite pleasing on the eye. I could imagine myself taking a relaxing stroll along there one day.

There isn't anywhere near the amount of building work going on, even though they are busy preparing for the Asian Games, which are supposed to start in a month or two. There aren't half as many huge, ego-boosting buildings sprouting from every available scrap of land. There isn't as much neon. They still drive like maniacs, yes, but in this part of the world it seems that insurance is provided by *Allah*.

There are many more what you might call Arabic-influenced buildings there. They seem to be obsessed with a horned animal called an Oryx, and even have a cuddly animated version as a mascot for the games. The other local obsession seems to be jugs, pearls and oysters, with references galore in bar names, development titles and giant sculptures featuring said oysters sitting in the middle of roundabouts. Oy, mate, your Venus is missing!

And yet, and yet...the insidious influence of Dubai is slowly coming to the fore. There are a number of shiny, new high-rise building projects at the West Bay end of the Corniche, including the one which I am involved in, and they are building a Pearl Island, rather than a Palm Island, just off the coast. It still has a lot of catching up to do, and I sincerely hope they rein this ambition in a bit, because if everywhere turns into Dubai, the whole Gulf region will turn into a giant Vegas wannabe without the gambling. Who wants that?

Maybe some people do, actually, because the expat people I have met so far in Doha seemed to be a tad bitter about the fact that they were there rather than Dubai, which meant they had the choice of a handful of malls, hotels and bars to frequent, and not much else. It was difficult not to feel smug about the fact that I was going back to Dubai.

As it happened, I ended up staying more time than I was meant to, because the meeting about the Big Hole in the Ground ended up spawning more meetings about the Big Hole in the Ground, and the client decided I was needed there the next day. Oh, joy. Before I had a chance to object, my company's Dubai office had changed my flight and booked me into the Doha Marriot.

After the meetings ended I was given a lift back along the Corniche to my hotel by the wiry-framed, pipe-smoking South African site quantity surveyor, who took the opportunity to moan at me about the job and the country all the way there. When we arrived, another notable difference to Dubai became immediately apparent:

there were security checkpoints and road barriers outside the hotel, and just inside the main doors there was an airport-style X-ray machine and walk-through metal detector. I found this slightly disconcerting to say the least. To me it said quite bluntly: "Western Hotels are potential targets". Despite Dubai being the diametric opposite of places like Saudi Arabia in terms of religious strictness, there haven't been any major terrorist attacks there. The theories (or wild rumours, I'm learning to call them) as to why this is the case range from terrorist groups being bribed to keep away to the police having one in four of the local populace as informants. It's hard to know what to believe, as it is a subject rarely talked about in wider public circles. As for Doha, I know there has been one isolated incident here to date, where a theatre frequented by Westerners was targeted by a lone nut-job, so all the security at the hotel seemed a little excessive to me.

Before checking in I spent an exasperating 20 minutes in the hotel gift shop buying a shirt, some underwear, cans of deodorant and the like. I had nothing other than the clothes I was wearing and a briefcase full of paperwork. I decided that fashioning some clothes out of these documents would probably not meet with my client's approval, so I was resigned to forking out some money. Finding my size was a Krytpon Factor-esque challenge. Some items were sold in European sizes and some were sold in US sizes, so I had to make educated guesses about what would fit my ample frame.

Later that night some of the people from various companies working on the job joined me at the hotel. These guys were really hardened expats...wise, yet world-weary, and with a penchant for a heady mix of alcohol and BS. We ate and drank heartily and talked about Big Holes in the Ground and Doha until my day caught up with me, so I made my excuses and headed for my room. I should have gone to sleep, but I did what I always do in hotel rooms and turned on the television. I laid on the King-sized bed and watched The Fast Show on the wonderful BBC Prime (a real gem of a channel for expats), then the first hour of the film Gladiator on another channel (which I've seen many times, but I still love it), before my heavy eyes made it impossible to watch any more, and I gave in to my need for sleep.

Next day, after a leisurely breakfast delivered to my room (chicken sausages and beef bacon, yummy!) and a shower, I put on the ill-fitting clothes that I'd bought in the gift shop and jumped feet first into another day of intrigue and mystery. Thankfully our meetings were concluded by lunchtime, and I was soon being conveyed back to the airport for my re-arranged flight back to Dubai. While I waited in the departure lounge I watched the surprisingly busy Doha airport runway, where planes of all sizes departed to and arrived from various exotic locations, including Bahrain, Kuala Lumpur, Bangkok and Manchester.

Boarding is via buses in Doha, but this still doesn't stop the agitated, bovine masses pushing and elbowing their way to the front of the queue when boarding is announced, as if it will get them to their destination any quicker. I've even heard tales of people in this part of the world getting out of their seat as the plane is on final approach and reaching for the overhead luggage bins to make sure they get off the plane first.

When we eventually boarded the Qatar Airways plane I wondered why they were using an Airbus A340, which is a large plane for such a short flight. It's possible that this plane was on a stop-over from somewhere else, as it soon filled up, mainly with Indians and Bangladeshis who seemed to have a huge problem with sitting in their assigned seats. Much head waggling and arm waving ensued, and, along with the late arrival of about another fifty people, this meant we took off nearly half an hour late.

I found myself glad to be back in Dubai. And despite the needlessly searching questions of the passport controller and the panicky few minutes when I forgot where I'd parked my car, I drove away feeling quite good about stuff. I even went back to the office for half an hour and caught up with the boss before he left for a two week holiday in the UK. I think he was surprised to see me, but it probably made a good impression.

I'm worried about it all. I'm enjoying the job. I'd almost given up on surveying quantities as a career, but coming here has shown me that it can be (reasonably) exciting and dynamic, especially when you're dealing with jobs of this nature, and you get to jet round the region, if not the world, seeing new places and meeting new people. I think I'm doing OK, and so far the boss seems happy with me. Fingers crossed - or *Insha'allah* as they say here - it will continue.

Saturday, September 16, 2006

Water, Water everywhere...

Watch out: It's time for a grumble. I've been mainly positive up to now, making out that life in Dubai is perfect. Well, maybe not, but it's about time I got something off my chest.

I read a statistic the other day - I can't remember where, probably in the local free tabloid called 7 Days (think of the UK's Metro) or possibly the Dubai version of Time Out magazine – which stated that the average daily consumption of water in the UAE is five hundred litres per *person*. That really is quite startling when you think about it. It's one of the highest rates, if not *the* highest in the world.

I started to think about my own contribution to this incredible figure: I drink maybe two litres a day, have a shower, go to the toilet a few times (I can't help biology), wash the dishes, etc., but FIVE HUNDRED LITRED? Come on. Then I thought about it the world outside my front door; what I've seen going on all around me, and I started to comprehend how this place uses so much.

When you drive around Dubai on a daily basis you see sprinklers everywhere. There is established and newly-planted grass all over the place, and in the heat of the desert summer it needs watering at least twice a day. Yes, sand is boring. Grass and greenery looks nice. So I kind of grudgingly accept it as being par for the course. Arf bloody arf. It's part of the whole experience here. You turn a blind eye to these excesses, and the liberal / environmental guilt is pushed to one side when you see the things that you see and hear about some of the stuff that goes on. It's the price you pay for coming to a place like this. But then some things just push you too far.

In the vast, Truman Show-style suburban sprawl that is Springs, I often come across large puddles and streams of water flowing across the streets, and wonder where it's coming from. I now have my answer. Today I spotted a hired hand (gardener / maid / servant) hosing down the block-paved carport area to the front of a villa. I drove by slowly and watched as this person nonchalantly ejected countless litres of water onto the paving, all with the supposed aim of clearing away the sand and dust that gathers in such areas. The street was a veritable river, and a big blob of wet sand was gathering in the gutter. Truly amazing, and a complete waste of water! Why not sweep the paving? The sand comes back, unerringly and inevitably, every single day, because, what do you know? We live in the desert and it's quite windy most of the time and so the hired hand has to repeat this task every few days, just so that the poor Sirs and Madams don't have to walk in a bit of sand. They probably wash the cars every day as well. Now I am starting to get an idea of where the five hundred litres goes.

All this makes me ponder the sanity of this place, because every week or so there are grim warnings in the press about how the water is going to run out soon. There have been shortages already in some, less well-off areas (*quelle surprise*), and the rate of growth here just boggles the mind. Where do they get it all from, and how are they going to supply all these developments? It's not just for human consumption, either. As well as the grass and trees, most of these developments have water features - man-made lakes and lagoons and huge centre-piece fountains or waterfalls.

In terms of domestic water it seems that most of the water here is from the sea and is desalinated. It is supposedly OK to drink, but everyone drinks bottled water, which is sold cheaply in the supermarkets or delivered to your home in large bottles if you have an office-style water-cooler, which can be bought in the supermarkets. I'd get one myself, but would worry about Teresa and kids congregating round it and gossiping about me.

Apparently, there are underground fresh water supplies, but they are apparently being depleted at an alarming rate. I really hope that the people in charge know what they're doing here, because it could all go horribly wrong if they don't rein in the ridiculous levels of consumption, especially of the kind that is completely and utterly unnecessary. Come on, it is. I can't think of one defence for it.

Monday, September 18, 2006

A Gecko's Tail.

We had a little visitor to our villa today. A tiny little gecko got in through a gap under the door and my wife let out a little yelp when she saw it scuttling around on the white, tiled floor. For me, reptiles are fine. Spiders are another matter with all those legs and eyes and hairy appendages. My wife tried to drop a plastic dish on top of it, but it managed to escape, leaving its tail behind, which proceeded to lie there and twitch for a good minute or more. Bizarre! My wife thought she'd cut it off with the dish, but it transpires that this is the natural defence mechanism of a gecko, which they can use when they feel threatened.

Mother Nature, I doff my cap, because it works. We were more interested in the still-moving tail than the little reptile. Meanwhile, Mr. Gecko was under the sofa, probably laughing at us silly humans. We finally managed to corner him when he re-emerged, and I scooped him up in a glass, took him outside and let the little chap go. Sorry for scaring you, Mr. Gecko, and I hope your tail grows back OK.

Friday, September 22, 2006

The Sun Always Shines

Well it has since I arrived those many weeks ago. I haven't seen many clouds. There have been a couple of sand-storms and a bit of fog for a couple of mornings, but apart from that, it has burned in the sky every single day. It is hot, bright, unforgiving, but is also the primary reason we are able to live on this planet. You've probably heard the figures about how many nuclear bomb's-worth of energy that big ball of gas produces.

We were out in it for a bit today. After a slightly disappointing brunch in Focaccia, an Italian restaurant in the Hyatt Regency on the Deira Corniche, we went for a little walk along the creek. We didn't go too far, as the sun is still very hot at this time of year, spending just enough time in the open air to get a feel for the area. This part of Dubai is visibly older and has fewer high-rise buildings, but you can see that this is where the city started taking off twenty or thirty years ago when you notice the newer, shinier buildings that have cropped up further down the creek. They aren't as big or as brash as the buildings on Sheik Zayed Road, but they point to the arrival of modern commerce in the area back in the 1970s and 80s. Of course, it goes even further back than that with the pearling and the sea-borne trade. There are still hundreds of traditionally-built wooden dhows in use and docked along the creek, all emptying or loading goods from Iran, India and further afield.

After our walk we set off towards home and it was then that Teresa remarked, "Why don't they use solar panels here?"

Good bloody question, my dear, and one which has crossed my mind more than once. All that free, unlimited (well, maybe for five billion years) energy, and the powers that be apparently haven't thought of using it.

I'm no expert in the field, so could be barking up the wrong palm tree here, but surely they wouldn't have to waste too much prime real estate ground. They could put solar panels on top of every single building without spoiling their aesthetics, and supply the staggering amount of juice that's needed for the 24/7 air conditioning alone.

As it is, the sun heats the domestic cold water in most buildings; in most cases it is stored in roof-top tanks, so you have a cold tap that runs hot and a hot tap giving you water from a boiler that is redundant for around five months of the year.

I suppose that saves a bit of electricity, but as I have previously alluded to, Dubai and the UAE are enormous consumers of resources. If this place was the size of the USA, we'd be nominating George Dubya Bush for honorary membership of Greenpeace. If it's not the A/C, it's the flashy, colour-changing lights that seem to decorate every building with more than ten storeys. Then there's the like of Ski Dubai. Keeping that incredible amount of space at sub-zero temperatures whilst it's knocking on fifty degrees centigrade outside must use an astonishing amount of energy. The poor bugger they have feeding fifty pence pieces into the meter must be knackered. So, what is the problem? Why not use solar power?

Is it maybe because we couldn't get charged very much for electricity that was produced by the sun? Who knows for sure? Do you? DEWA? Hmmm.

Ouch, the cynicism is starting to kick in, and I've not even been here two months...

Saturday, September 23, 2006

On the First Day of Ramadan

We didn't even know it had started until we got to the Ibn Battuta Mall and found that is was pretty much deserted. All the food outlets were closed; chairs tipped against or stacked on tables and serving windows silent and empty. The moon-watching committee must have spotted that new moon last night. My son, with his usual forthright manner, was asking all kinds of questions including: "Who is the man that looks out for the moon?" and, "What happens if he falls asleep and misses it?"

So we shopped at the hypermarket, taking in this new, unusual atmosphere. No people smoking or eating or drinking; melodic, enchanting Arabian music lilting gently from the speakers; westerners dressed like they're on the beach...some things never change.

This is the holiest time in the Islamic calendar. It changes dates every year depending on the phases of the moon and lasts four weeks. It culminates in the *Eid* festival at the end. During this time, Muslims must not eat, drink or smoke during daylight hours. I think there are a few other things they aren't allowed to do as well, but can't remember what exactly. It's all supposed to test their faith, purify their souls and remind them of others' plight; something like that.

It also affects non-Muslims, who are obliged to respect the feelings of the locals and avoid eating and drinking in public or in view of Muslims. This is why most food outlets are closed during the period, although some of the big hotels apparently have restaurants that are open behind closed doors. Alcohol is completely banned until sunset, or about 7pm, however.

After the food shopping was completed we went back home, had some lunch and decided to go and explore the Madinat Jumeirah. This is a vast tourist complex centred on a shopping mall in the style of a traditional souk. There are two large luxury hotels - one at either end - and a lower level with dozens of restaurants and man-made waterways winding their way all around the complex. *Abras* (little wooden water taxis) transport people around these fake rivers, from the hotel to the souk and back. As was the case in the mall, there were no food outlets open, and very few people around. We felt a bit like intruders, but enjoyed snooping around in the eerie quiet and enjoyed the jaw-dropping views of the pristine, sail-shaped Burj Al Arab that greeted us around every other corner. It's truly another world.

After leaving the Madinat we drove to the public beach on the other side of the Burj Al Arab. We parked alongside a low concrete wall that separated the road from the beach and I took the kids down onto the beach for a quick paddle in the freakily warm waters of the Arabian Gulf. While we paddled, we watched two helicopters land on the heli-pad at the top of the hotel, which was pretty cool. The kind of people who use a helicopter to get to such a place must be just unspeakably, obscenely rich.

The disappointing thing about the beach was that it was quite dirty. There were cigarette ends by the million near the wall, and I even spotted a discarded dirty nappy. It was relatively quiet, but there were a few hardy souls there, soaking up the still-scorching afternoon sun. I've heard stories of Indian or Pakistani men who go to these public beaches just to stand and stare at the acres of exposed female flesh, while engaging in a not-so-subtle game of pocket billiards. When you realise that these guys come from rural villages in India and have never seen a woman in a bikini, you kind of see why they behave like that, but things like this and the dirtiness of the beach take the sheen of the place. I think that's why a lot of people use the beach parks and clubs where you have to pay to get in. I think they look after them much better. Here's hoping, anyway!

OCTOBER

Monday, October 02, 2006

Birthday, Boredom, Baldness, Blobbiness.

Please have violins and muted trumpets ready: I'm officially having my first bad week here in Dubai. I'm getting a cold, I turned thirty-six just over a week ago, and then I found out that I have put about a stone on in the two months that I've been here. Woe, woe and thrice whoa! I suppose that's what happens when someone cuts you a small slice of chocolate birthday cakes, but you take the big bit and leave what's left for rest of the family to share.

Ramadan is still going on and on. The working days are shorter (well, supposedly - we work till 4pm with no lunch break, but I'm often there till 4.30 or 5pm - these boss people ain't stupid). The Malls are bizarre: no cigarette smoke, no bustle in cafés and restaurants, just vacant tables and seats, as if you are there in the middle of the night or in a George Romero zombie flick set in Arabia. Heck, some people here drive like zombies right now, probably due to their low energy levels from the fasting. You see them drooling on their phones as they zoom past you at 180kph to get home for *iftar* (the breaking of the fast at sunset).

I digress...I was talking about the malls. We went to the Mall of the Emirates on Friday to look for shoes for Joseph, but it turned out he didn't need new ones just yet. That was a bonus. If only he could stay that size. Then we went looking for nourishment, which is a difficult task during Ramadan, as you may imagine. We walked past the giant windows looking in on the other-worldly snowy expanse of Ski Dubai to the Kempinski Hotel end of the Mall...

...and the mall-level restaurants were all closed, despite Time Out Dubai saying that at least one of them would be open for brunch. Useless gets. I should have realised their info was unreliable after their frankly questionable review of Foccacia at the Hyatt Regency. Anyway, I remembered that there was this place called Sezzam in the Kempinski, and we found it down on the ground level after another white-knuckle ride down an escalator with two kids and a push-chair. The restaurant was hidden behind black curtains running the length of the lobby, keeping the gobbling hordes out of sight, away from those who are fasting. Seems fair, I suppose. I wouldn't like to watch people eat if I wasn't allowed to eat for fourteen hours.

The food was pretty good, after all that. The grilled bratwurst the only thing that wasn't really good, it wasn't a real bratwurst - far too soft, and lacking flavour, but the lamb chops (more like a half-rack) were heavenly, as was the cheesy mash and the grilled veg. Teresa had Tandoori chicken, which tasted really nice and fresh and not at all dry (although she said there was too much coriander...never bloody happy), and Joseph and Emma ate their pizza and nuggets with little complaint. Emma's fresh fruit salad also impressed. This is turning into a restaurant review, isn't it? While I'm here, then, I would also say that the service is a bit patchy, but friendly. I will definitely return.

So Saturday came, and we ended up in a bloody shopping mall again. This time it was Ibn Battuta (Joseph has asked if he had a massive hooter), which is actually a very unusual mall, because it has separate themed areas. I took the family for a little wander in there to see the different zones and the things you just don't expect to see in malls, like full-size replicas of Chinese junks and elephants with enormous tusks.

We did the weekly shop in the Géant hypermarket, which we seem to have settled upon as the best place. Carréfour in MOE is just too manic, Spinneys is too small and expensive, but Géant seems to have it sorted, except they don't have a pork section, so we always end up going to Spinneys or Choithrams for the much-needed bacon and ham, etc. I'm just glad we don't live in Saudi or Qatar, where pork is completely banned. I'm a pig-product lover, and proud of it.

Shopping for food is always a soul-destroying experience, in my view. Up and down with the trolley with two whingeing kids in tow... so you have to make it interesting by throwing surprise items into the trolley - usually nice-tasting, fattening items, it must be said – or trying to knock pyramids of canned vegetables over accidentally on purpose.

Food, glorious food...ah, yes: the solution to and cause of all my problems. (so says a certain Homer J Simpson, but referring to beer). I obviously can't live without it, but I'm living too much through it. I am in that horrible cycle of eating, feeling fat, not sleeping, feeling shite, eating to feel better, feeling fat, and so on.... I need to snap out of it before I break the twenty stone barrier. SNAP OUT OF IT, MAN!

So what did I do? I looked at exercise bikes for maybe fifteen seconds, but ended up buying a PS2 because Joseph and I need our Pro Evolution Soccer fix. Teresa is now resigned to watching us replaying Boro v Sevilla over and over again to avenge that horrible UEFA Cup Final humiliation. And then she has to listen to Joseph's crying and my shouting when we play Tekken 4 (it came free with the console), because we're both terrible losers. I particularly hate losing to people who just randomly mash the controller buttons.

Talking of the Boro...they're depressing me as well! Bloody hell! Losing to Sheffield frigging United (with all due respect).

AAAGGGGGHHH!

I think it could cabin fever, actually. Our lives are just a procession of moving between villa, car, office, car, mall, car, hotel and back to villa. I just want this damn weather to cool down enough for us to get outside for a decent length of time!

Whinge over. *Alhamdulillah*!

Sunday, October 08, 2006
Take Me Higher

If you drive along the Sheik Zayed Road toward the creek from the Marina, as you head towards the Trade Centre area with all the glittering, high-rise skyscrapers, you can't help but notice what is being built on the right hand side.

The Burj Dubai will be over eight hundred metres tall (half a mile!) and will have one hundred and sixty two floors (maybe more), and will be the tallest building in the world (by a long chalk) when finished in 2 or 3 years' time. Taipei 101, the current highest at around five hundred metres, will be a tiddler in comparison.

I've seen it many times - I pass it on my way to work every day, and it's almost perceptibly changing week by week. It's already the biggest building in Dubai, currently standing at seventy four floors, and they are building it at a rate of a floor a week, which means they should be done in about another eighty eight weeks, by my reckoning. Then there's just...*just*...the outer cladding and the internal works to do.

It doesn't really look that big from a distance, but when you get up close, you appreciate what a massive beast it is - and will be. According to information gleaned from the internet, it's not even close to half-way completed in height terms. I managed to get close to it last Thursday - eventually - because I had to go and see a man about another tall building (the one in Doha that I'm working on), and he just happens to work in a site office that is situated at the foot of the Burj.

The other staggering thing about it is the development going on all around it. It's like a town in itself, with other towers and malls and parks and Lord only knows what else. The very plush sales and marketing building (a substantial development in its own right) to one side was easy to find, but I managed to get lost trying to find the site office right next to the tower, which sounds ridiculous considering the size of it, but the actual development has one small site entrance which isn't that easy to find if you're a relative Dubai newbie like me. But I think what I'm trying to say is...IT'S BLOODY HUGE!

During my research on the internet I came across a list of the tallest buildings and structures in the world. It included some of the proposed new structures that are in the pipeline, and I soon realised that the Burj Dubai is looking like a model of Canary Wharf in comparison to what is being planned. They are talking about building one in Kuwait that will be one kilometre high, but that is still dwarfed by the proposed Murjan Tower in Bahrain, which will be twenty-two metres higher, and will have two hundred floors. Truly mind-boggling.

Not only do you wonder how they can possibly build something so high (you take your hats off to the engineers, never an easy thing for a QS to do), you wonder about the logistics surrounding such a structure. What would happen to people on the two-hundredth floor if a fire broke out on the tenth? It would take about two hours to descend via the stairs. Are they planning to provide parachutes or death slides attached to other buildings? You won't get me up one of them, that's for sure. On a recent visit to Paris I got as far as the first floor of the Eiffel Tower and was pretty much begging my wife to let me go back down. I just don't feel safe unless there is nice, firm, safe land all around - and level – with me.

It seems this part of the world has become obsessed with building the biggest of everything now. They've made a heap of money from oil, and want to spend it by playing with life-size Mecanno sets, trying to outdo their neighbours. You have to wonder where it will end...when they reach the moon, perhaps.

Wednesday, October 11, 2006
Never Again

We all say it when we're hung over, but we always end up going back to booze, like we go back to the slightly mad lover who gives us great sex but then beats us up with a large frozen sausage afterwards. Or is that just me?

I went out with some chaps from work last night to a very nice bar called Scarlett's, situated in the promenade at the bottom of the Emirates Towers. It was the first time I had actually been for a drink with anyone from work. As I've mentioned before, the staff at the company don't seem keen on fraternising outside of working hours, but this had been organised by the management as some kind of team-building/morale-boosting event.

I arrived quite early (Teresa wanted to get home and get the kids to bed after dropping me off) and stood at the bar for about half an hour, drinking a leisurely pint of Guinness and eating the nasty cheesy nuts provided for me by the bar staff (I trust the cheesy taste was meant to be there, and hadn't been added by unhygienic men who'd just been to the bathroom). I watched people coming and going, and being the nosey get I am, listened to odd snippets of conversations.

People watching can be quite interesting in Dubai; you see people of every nationality, dressed in so many different ways, speaking many different languages. And being the shallow being you are, you imagine what they do and what they are like. Anyone wearing a sharp suit and flashing their blackberry around is immediately labelled a complete fucking poser; any group of giggling females are probably Trolley Dollies; and any single bloke nursing a pint is a desperate loner with evil intent lurking behind an inoffensive exterior. Oh. That'll be me then.

Before long, the boss turned up. He said hello to me and also to the guy stood right behind me, who happened to be from my company. He had been actually there when I arrived, and we had stood there at the bar completely oblivious to our common employer, in complete silence for thirty minutes. He works on site; I work in the office so I'd never seen him before. There's perhaps some kind of quantum mechanical phenomenon that could describe this situation. Or quite probably there isn't.

Soon enough we were joined by the rest of the gang. The boss had his credit card prised from his cold, dead hands, and the tab was up and running. Guinness followed Guinness. I soon lost count. I got talking to the other new guys who have been joining the company in their droves recently. With all of two months under my belt, I felt like an old hand when I talked to the newest arrival, fresh off the plane only last week.

"Oh, yeah," I said, "Dubai this, Doha that...price of formwork - terrible inflation...bibble....really dodgy bars in Bur Dubai....bobble...have you been to Ski Dubai? Yadda yadda..."

After pint four or five I had an orange juice to pace myself and to prevent what could turn into a next-day atrial fibrillation episode if I wasn't careful. The quizzical looks were soon shot my way, along with the comical and the condescending remarks. Can't handle your drink, eh? So the next OJ had some vodka in it. Call me an easily-lead weak-minded fool, if you must. Obi-Wan would have a field day with me. These aren't the quantities you're looking for....

Then I had two Coronas, not coronaries, and a few snacks were ordered in a moment of the munchies. Before too long I was too drunk and too tired to carry on, but sober enough to know that I should make my way home. So I said my goodbyes, shook everyone's hand - even those who weren't in our group - and got a taxi home.

This morning was a bit of an ordeal and involved two important meetings: sod's law. On the way to meeting number one the traffic lights failed at the Trade Centre roundabout just as I was approaching them. In the meetings themselves lots of concentration was required in case I had to answer a question. The client Project Manager went a bit berserk over some of my figures at meeting number two. It was a long, long old day. So now I'm off to bed.

Friday, October 13, 2006
Ha-ha in Hatta

I read a label on a bottle of disinfectant today. It said, in that commanding manner that all these things seem to have, "KEEP AWAY FROM CHILDREN"

Good advice, I thought. Problem is, I've spawned two of them and so struggle to keep away from them for long periods of time.

Of course I love them really. There's Joseph: an inquisitive, sulky, boisterous, completely bonkers six-year-old who is inclined of late to impersonate Nelson Muntz from the Simpsons should anything unfortunate occur to anyone, particularly me. In the supermarket today I managed to knock a large bag of crisps off the shelf and onto the floor in my usual clumsy way.

"Ha-ha!"

Then I picked them up and dropped them again, just as I was about to replace them.

"HA-HA!"

He actually pointed at me when he laughed this time. I had to laugh as well, because the crab sandwich in my basket wasn't heavy enough to cause sufficient damage.

Then there's Emma. She's also bonkers – maybe even more so – and has the biggest case of split personality I've ever seen in a two-year-old. She will be making us laugh with her silly faces and voices and sounds one minute; the next she will be screaming and crying at some perceived injustice. This can cause some tense moments in restaurants and supermarkets, mainly because we have learned that it's best just to let her get on with it. Asking her to calm her down is about as effective as using cream cheese as a tile adhesive. The only really effective way of bringing a swift end to the tantrums and screaming is to threaten her teddy with an automatic weapon, but since this is frowned upon by do-gooding types and the public at large, we end up distracting her with silly songs and face-pulling. We invariably leave any public space we visit with our reputations as good parents and normal, balanced people in tatters.

Anyway, I'm digressing. We had a good day today, as it happens. Well, apart from the shouting match I had with Teresa when I mistakenly sent her the wrong way driving out of the Mall of the Emirates...it's an easy thing to do when the signs all point the wrong bloody way. Apart from *that* it was a good day. We did our food shop at Carrefour, had lunch, and then decided to head for Hatta. Hatta is a small town near the Omani border, about a hundred clicks from downtown Dubai. Getting there involves driving through the desert, albeit on a proper dual carriageway, and we fancied exploring a bit more of the country, so off we went.

As we left Dubai on the Oman-bound highway, we zipped by countless developments and hoarding heralding upcoming developments. We saw the full-sized replica space shuttle and roller coaster near where they are building Dubailand, which is naturally going to be bigger than Disneyland when it's finished. We saw a hoarding with a picture of a replica Eiffel tower. We saw the newly-started Sports City site, which will basically be an Olympic city (They haven't bid for the Olympics yet, but I don't doubt that they harbour such an ambition). We saw the recently-completed Autodrome: a Formula One-standard motor racing circuit standing there waiting for action in the middle of the desert. It just keeps going and going, and you realise that this place will (probably) still be growing in ten years.

Finally, we were leaving the mega-developments behind us. The landscape changed gradually as we got further into the wilds of the UAE. The plant life became more and more scarce, the sand darkened in colour, and about forty-five minutes after setting off, we were on a pristine highway surrounded by undulating orange dunes and not very much else, really. A game of I Spy would have lasted about four rounds... road...sand...car...OK, three rounds. The traffic was virtually non-existent, and every way we looked there was just ochre sand and azure sky.

This continued for a while, and then we spotted the mountain range coming into view on the horizon. These mountains are real desert mountains - grey, harsh, inhospitable and impressive in scale. They looked like the mountains in Lord of the Rings. Sound the trumpets! Bilbo Bobbins is coming!

As I was taking in this view, an SMS came through to my mobile telling me I could use my Etisalat account on a roaming basis. Which is all well and good, but I thought I was still in the UAE. Wrong! It transpires that you actually go into Oman and then out again on the way to Hatta, which is part in the Emirate of Dubai. My phone was now telling me that my network was Etisalat Oman. Crazy shit, man. There were no border controls or any signs saying WELCOME TO OMAN in English or squiggly Arabic writing or anything...not that I would have understood the Arabic, of course. They do have different petrol stations, though. I saw a Shell garage for the first time in three months. I was nearly overcome with excitement and wanted to stop and buy a stale, over-priced sandwich, a large bag of jelly babies and a can of de-icer. The wife wouldn't let me. She's always spoiling my fun.

We had read about the carpet shops along the road to Hatta in one of the expat guides, and lo and behold, there is a long stretch of roller-shutter-fronted low buildings that sell carpets as you approach Hatta. Teresa was keen to find a nice rug for the living room, so we pulled in at one and after a quick look around and the obligatory haggle (you've gotta haggle), we drove away with a nice colourful rug.

Then we arrived in Hatta. You know you've got to Hatta because you come to a roundabout with a big mock fort thing right in the middle of it. It's called Hatta Fort, of all things. They are into literalism round here.

Hatta itself is pretty unimpressive. There are lots of shabby buildings strewn around and they have the biggest speed bumps in the world. It is hilly, which makes a change from the uniform flatness of Dubai, I suppose. There is a heritage site there as well, but it looked closed, so we headed to the Hatta Fort Hotel, which is raved about in various publications. It's more like a resort than a hotel, with sporting facilities galore and chalet style rooms. We had a play in the kiddies' park, a quick gurn at the beautiful people in the inviting pools, and then as we walked around the hotel grounds, we turned round at just the right moment and caught sight of the view that was behind us as we entered the main hotel building. The craggy mountains were now set in dark profile against a reddening sky as the sun made its way towards the horizon. It was a stunning view, and on its own made the trip worth it.

Before going home we went for tea in the hotel coffee shop - or dinner, whatever you wanna call it. It was getting late, and there was an hour and a half's drive ahead. The meal was OK. Not over-expensive and not really flash. Adequate is the word I'm looking for. What made it for us was having a really good view of the sun setting behind the mountains as we ate. Joseph was particularly impressed as he saw the last sliver of burning orange disappear behind the mountain.

To be fair, the banana and coconut pie was really nice.

So, we left Hatta in the dark. I was quite excited about this, because I fully expected to drive back to Dubai through the desert and see the starry, unpolluted sky above me, which is supposedly a really awesome sight to behold. Sadly, this wasn't to be, because the oh-so-safety conscious people running this country decided to put great big, bright orange street lights along the entire length of the

Dubai to Hatta highway, so all we saw above our heads on the drive back was a procession of street lights passing overhead like a line of UFOs on their way to the Mall of Mars. It didn't even feel slightly dangerous or anything, because it was like driving along an urban motorway back in the "civilised West". They can do thousands and thousands of street lights - oh yes. But can they stop people driving like maniacs? I think you know the answer.

As for the starry sky – I hope that our time will come. A desert safari trip is going to have to be squeezed in at some point. Then we should be able to get away from lights and noise and mad driving and maybe see that sky. I can't wait.

Tuesday, October 17, 2006

A Sad State of Affairs

I heard something a bit sad yesterday. Apparently, there is a local company that runs a particular petrol station (there are only three or four companies in the UAE) that not only pays their pump attendants a pittance (like most service providers), it also takes their tips away from them. These guys stand in the heat all day, filling our cars and washing our windscreens, and are probably seen as little better than livestock by most of the people here.

They do get given tips, though. If the tank of petrol costs, say sixty-six dirhams (less than a tenner), you generally give them seventy and let them keep the change. It's not much, I know, but the assumption would be that they use these tips to supplement their meagre wages. Not so, if the reports are true. Apparently, said petrol station firm orders their workers to hand over the tips to the company. They have no pockets in their uniform trousers and it has reportedly been known for the company to search these guys before they go home at the end of their shifts. If it's true, it's disgusting and vile and utterly greedy, and I will do my best to avoid using this company's filling stations again.

This place ain't perfect; far from it.

Saturday, October 21, 2006

On The Last Day of Ramadan

Which is...when, exactly?

It's a bit of a guessing game, it seems. The country is getting all geared up for *Eid Al Fitr* and the long weekend, but the lack of announcements in the press (no 7 Days newspaper delivered today) means we are in a state of limbo. We don't know if Ramadan is over or not, especially as it started early, according the expat grapevine. I told Teresa that she should run down to the Town Centre shopping centre to see if Starbucks was open or if the mosque was surrounded by a million badly-parked cars. That would tell us for sure. She told me to bog off.

We went to yet another shopping mall yesterday - the Burjuman Centre in Bur Dubai. It was dead; quieter than the trophy room at St. James' Park. More than half the shops were closed, along with all the food outlets and the kids' play areas. The shops that were open were almost universally bereft of shoppers, with bored-looking assistants sitting at their counters staring at their mobile phones and wishing their lives away. Is this what happens at the end of Ramadan? My lack of knowledge on these matters is frustrating, but it seems that it's the way of the world round here. Holidays are based on the movements and sightings of the moon, so they can be announced with very little notice at all. I've been told several tales of people going to work and finding out they shouldn't have bothered.

Anyway....we're going to Wild Wadi today, which is a water park between the Burj Al Arab and the Jumeirah Beach Hotel. It should be fun, as long as I don't end up getting wedged in one of the slide tubes. I've rung ahead and they told me that the Ramadan restrictions aren't enforced in the park, and all the concession areas are open for business, which makes sense really. You couldn't expect people to visit an outdoor amusement park without access to at least drinks.

I will report back later.

Sunday, October 22, 2006

The Last Day of Ramadan? It's Today

The boys in charge have decided in their wisdom that today is the last day of Ramadan and tomorrow is that start of *Eid Al Fitr*, so the fasting ends and the partying begins. Phew. I say "Phew," and I wasn't even fasting. My suspicions appear to have been right and they *did* declare Ramadan early this year, so it was actually one day longer than normal.

So yesterday we had a day out, as I mentioned before, and went to the water park called Wild Wadi. We didn't tell the kids about it until we got there. Joseph was convinced we were destined for another half-empty shopping mall. We even sneaked the swimming bags into the car while he had his attention elsewhere. As we got closer to the park he started to suspect the truth and he could barely conceal the relief and excitement in his voice.

We had a really good time. There were plenty of rides and slides for young and old; gentle ones and wild ones; wave pools and climbing frames. I found out that the biggest attraction in the park is a very high and very steep slide called the *Jumeirah Sceirah*. I even made my way to the upper area of the park where it is located, but when I caught sight of the queue winding all the way down the tower and out onto the terrace at the bottom, I changed my mind. I didn't chicken out, honest.

I decided to have a go on the ride that goes all the way round the park, with the rider sitting in a large rubber ring which floats in a narrow half-pipe. It goes up, down, left, right, over bridges and through long, dark tunnels. There were really powerful water jets to propel you on the upward sections of the ride, which is pretty impressive when you're nearly twemty stone. The only problem with this is that the jets had a habit of catching my shorts and pushing them off my backside. I'm glad that none of the slide sections were see-through, for the sake of those below me. It was pretty damn cool, anyway. I liked the way I was able to choose different routes of varying scariness on the way and have a different journey every time.

Joseph was a bit shy with some of the bigger things, but was eventually encouraged to go into the wave pool, and had to be literally dragged out of it when we left. Emma was her usual Jekyll and Hyde mix of giggling fun and gibbering hysteria. I don't think she should have tried the *Sceirah* by herself, personally.

Possibly the strangest sight in the park was seeing some of the women (locals and Indians) who went on the rides in full clothing. They obviously have cultural and religious issues with modesty, but it was still quite peculiar seeing women in ornate saris and abbayas whizzing along various water flumes. Those things must weigh a ton when they are wet.

As the sun started to set, we made our way out of the park. As we neared the changing rooms, the Wadi Show was gearing up. They have built this large artificial cliff-face with a little *wadi* at the bottom (a *wadi* being a desert valley that is dry most of the time but is prone to flash floods when there are rainstorms). As we were walking past, thunder crashed from the speakers at ear-splitting levels, and the kids weren't too happy about that, I can tell you. Then the water started spilling from the top of the cliff, followed by a torrent of water that came rushing down the cliff, flooding the *wadi*. I suppose it's meant to mimic what happens in real *wadis*.

When I told Joseph this, he asked me in a shaky voice if there were any near our house. I used my best fatherly tone to reassure him that the only real ones existed out in the desert near the mountains. This didn't really convince him to stay and watch, especially with the colossal noise, so we quickly entered the changing rooms and got ready to leave. Teresa and Emma had long gone.

Overall, Wild Wadi is a pretty good place to go for a day out, I would say, especially as a family or in big groups. I particularly like the little innovation of the wristbands that get you in and out of the park, open and lock the lockers, and store credit on them which can be spent in the food outlets around the park so you don't have to carry money around. You get any unused money back at the end. There are some good rides, loads of catering outlets (slightly expensive, as is the norm, I suppose - but not outrageously so) and plenty of places with loungers and parasols to sit and relax if that's what you want to do. And I didn't get stuck in any tubes – they have allowed for the more portly gentleman, which is nice.

After the wildness of the *wadi*, we headed for a burger at Hardees and then, in a moment of impulse, decided to go for a coffee and a *shisha*, (sometimes called a hubbly-bubbly or *nargile*). We went to the Madinat, which was the closest place I thought we could find some, and after a bit of a trek around the Madinat souk, we found out that they had a *shisha* terrace at the Mina A'Salam hotel, which is one of two five-star hotels at either end of the complex.

We wandered in to the plush reception, wearing shorts and t-shirts and looking slightly bedraggled from our soggy adventures, and were lead to the terrace by one of the hotel staff without any hint of haughtiness. It's obviously an everyday occurrence in these parts. We sat under a gazebo on large comfy chairs and ordered a strawberry-flavoured *shisha* and some drinks. The *shisha* man set up the big bong-like contraption and set it going with the hot coals he kept in a special oven off to one side, before bringing it over and puffing at the end of the pipe to make sure it was lit. Then he stuck a clean plastic pipe in the end and handed it to us.

Teresa was curious - I've tried *shisha* before in Taiwan, of all places - so she had a few little drags on it. After a couple of splutters and coughs she admitted it was quite pleasant - and it is. The smoke is thick, but cool, tasty and very smooth; nothing like a cigarette or cigar. The water takes the harshness out of the smoke.

After about five minutes I had a mild buzz, but tobacco always does that to me. Teresa had nearly as much of it as I did, but the best bit was her comical expression when she smoked. Her eyebrows shot up and her eyes widened, and then she turned her head quickly to one side before exhaling. I laughed every time she took a pull.

The drinks were really nice as well. I had a Kiwi Cooler mocktail which was cool, refreshing and bursting with real fruit flavours. The kids were happy to wander around our gazebo, sipping their drinks and looking out over the balcony at the little water taxis (*abras*) coming and going from the station below us. Joseph even wanted a try at the *shisha*, but we couldn't get him to suck instead of blow, so all he did was make smoke come out of the other end. I don't think the *shisha* man was impressed with us letting our six-year-old smoke, but like all good politicians, he didn't inhale.

We finished our drinks, paid our bill and went down to the *abra* station. The Madinat has artificial waterways all around it, with little *abras* to transport guests around the complex. The boats are meant to be for hotel guests only, but they weren't to know, and I doubt we're the first to buck the system, so we jumped on one and glided smoothly past the waterfront promenades full of people dining under the Arabian skies. Gentle mood lighting and ethnic music adding to the holiday atmosphere; a gentle, warm breeze caught our faces, and, "Oh, this is the life," is probably the thought that drifted languidly through our collective minds. Or in the case of Emma, "I hope Dora the Explorer is on TV when we get home".

Monday, October 23, 2006
Eid Mubarak

As they say in these parts.

It means Happy *Eid*, and I think everyone is happy that Ramadan is over. The locals are happy because they can stop the fasting, the early mornings and the late nights, and the rest of us are happy because we can get a coffee or a sandwich while we're out and about during the day. Oh, we are such superficial, desperate beings.

It's been an extraordinary experience, and very educational. Without wanting to sound trite, I think a lot of people could learn from being in a place like this during Ramadan. In most cases (not all, it has to be said), concessions and allowances are made, mutual respect is shown, and we all muddle through somehow.

Of course, people still find things to bicker about, and it's a shame that the bickering seems to be getting quite nasty back in the UK. The whole issue of ladies wearing the veil is highlighting the divisions and the intolerance that can bubble away beneath the surface of any multi-cultural society. Point-scoring and one-upmanship is rife, on all sides.

Sometimes, when I'm at a particularly low ebb, or have had a few too many drinks, I think there's no hope for humankind, because try as we might, a lot of us just can't accept differences or see things from other people's perspectives. But at other times I see great kindness and togetherness, and think that we aren't so bad after all. I know: I'm going off on one again. I try to keep this kind of thing out of here, but it is hard to avoid it when the issue affects your daily existence.

Today we had a little drive out, and after remarking on the quietness of the roads, we noticed that there were sub-continental chaps all over the place. They seemed to be at every major junction of every major road, even when we were out in the middle of nowhere on the Emirates Road, and almost every single one of them were resplendent in their Sunday best (or is it Friday best here?), with crisply ironed Carrefour shirts and neatly-combed hair. We wondered who they were and what they were doing out there.

Were they the labourers finally getting some time off and heading out for the day? If so, how did they get to these places in the relative wilderness and to what end? And where were they going now? As we passed the huge Chinese discount mall called Dragon Mart (which was closed at the time), we saw a group of several dozen of these smartly-dressed men standing around near the entrance. There were no women or children there, or none that I could see.

Our drive took us towards the creek again, so we headed to a little theme park inside the Creekside Park, which is just over the Garhoud Bridge on the south side of the creek. This was closed as well, and again there was a small group of these men milling around. We finally landed at the Wafi City mall, which was open, and had a spot of lunch and a little play in the amusement area. There weren't any of these smartly-dressed sub-con men in here. I've heard that they don't let them in the big malls. Is this elitist or even racist? Who knows? Who decides? There were plenty of Emiratis there, also dressed in their best finery. The men's' dish-dashes were whiter and brighter than ever, and almost all of them were in a chipper mood. I saw two smiling young men played chess at one of the now-open coffee shops, laughing and joking to themselves all the while, while some younger men ran amok in the amusement areas, playing some kind of tag game or something like that. Large groups of women in their bejewelled, black robes and designer sunglasses browsed in the high-end fashion joints of the mall.

We headed home after the mall - the roads weren't much busier - and decided to go for a swim at our local communal pool. It was largely deserted when we arrived, but a few more people joined us later. We had a good old splash around in the warm afternoon sunshine, until, with sunset approaching, the flies started emerging in large numbers, and we headed home for tea.

Now I'm nicely tired again, and I've somehow managed to write a long entry again. Maybe not the most interesting or exciting one, but I hope it conveys something of the first day of *Eid*. It's back to work tomorrow, but there are only three days till the weekend comes round again.

Sunday, October 29, 2006

Rain, Rain......COME BACK!!!

We nearly, *nearly* saw rain on Friday. It's strange how you start to miss these kinds of things. I'll be missing cheeky-chappy chavs standing outside the shops asking politely for a cigarette next.

The point being, we haven't seen any since we arrived here. For me, that's three months without a hint of precipitation, which is something totally alien to someone hailing from the United Kingdom's verdant, lush, frequently-irrigated-from-the-sky pastures.

Anyway, to cut a short story long, we headed to the border with Oman on Friday with the express purpose of getting our visit visas renewed. They run out after sixty days, which meant we had to leave the UAE and come back again. Flying out of the country was one option, but I much preferred the option of driving, so we drove out through the desert again on the nearly-empty, brand-new highway and past loads of camels towards Hatta, carrying straight on over the fort roundabout and between the mountains towards the border, which is about another ten kilometres along the road.

As we approached the mountains, we noticed that there were big cloud formations just beyond. They looked like rain clouds - big, bright and bulbous *cumulus nimbus* with a menacing grey under-belly. Excitement grew in the family unit. We were actually looking forward to seeing some rain; maybe even going outside in it and dancing in it like madmen. As it was, we missed the rain. We arrived at the Omani passport checkpoint facility about twenty minutes too late, I reckon. The car-park tarmac was wet from a recent downpour, and the clouds were busy making their way into Oman. Ho-hum.

The border crossing and visa renewal process was, well...frustrating. We passed through three separate border control points on the way to Oman, and the same three on the way back. There was a UAE passport point, followed by an Omani customs point and then the Omani passport checkpoint about five kilometres after the customs point.

We weren't actually sure if we could drive into Oman, because our car hire company had completely bamboozled us by trying to sell us insurance to drive there then telling us we couldn't drive in Oman with UK licences. The border points themselves had very little in the way of visible information about what to do and where to go, so there was a lot of guesswork, stupid-question-asking, and wild gesticulation from heavily-armed border guards, whose menacing presence is a blessing to parents with fidgety, whiny kids.

After getting stamped out of the UAE, which involved getting out of the car and queuing at the window of a little white hut, we just sort of muddled our way past customs, buying insurance at the little office located on completely the wrong side of the road, then driving onwards not knowing what to do next.

We finally came across the passport control checkpoint, which is a large, brand-new building in the middle of nowhere. Again, there were no signs telling us what to do, so we parked the car in the puddles created by the recent rain and entered the building to find a large gaggle of confused-looking people queuing at various windows. Most of these people were expats doing the same thing as us. There were more border guards, with even bigger guns, milling around, keeping an eye out for naughty children.

After standing in one queue for a couple of minutes I struck up a conversation with the British chap in front of me, and learned that I had to queue at a different window to get some forms and pay the visa fees, then fill in the forms and queue at another window for the stamps, then get in the car and queue up to get into Oman. This is a common feature of this part of the world; nothing can be done in one place or in one go. You invariably end up queuing at three separate locations to get anything official done. It was the same when I had to go and open an account with DEWA for the electricity and water, and it's the same for a driving licence, evidently. I'm surprised I haven't had to queue at four different windows and fill in a dozen forms in triplicate just to get some baked beans with pork sausages.

Eventually we got our forms; paying two hundred and forty dirhams for the pleasure (the man did say a hundred and twenty to begin with, and then seemed to change his mind for some mysterious reason. I'll have to get that MUG tattoo lasered off). I filled the forms in, queued for the stamps, got back in the car and then drove to the wrong window, after trying to guess the right one and getting it ever-so-predictably wrong. They let us through anyway, and we did a quick U-turn through the car park on the Oman side and queued again to get the exit stamps. That was the easy bit, and we were back in no-man's land after our shortest visit ever to any country - all of two minutes. I'm glad we paid for that insurance.

There was yet more standing around and queuing at the UAE border, but the actual process was fairly painless there. The man behind the window at the very basic checkpoint stamped us back in without any searching questions about the flying speeds of swallows, and we finally re-entered the United Arab Emirates nearly two hours after leaving.

We were ready to drop, so I'm glad that we had had the foresight to book ourselves in for the night at the Hatta Fort Hotel, which we've visited before. Five minutes back into the UAE we pulled into the hotel grounds. A smiling, short man called Maxwell brought us delicious and refreshing fruit punch drinks while we checked in, before showing us to our chalet-style room. It was cosy and nicely-furnished with a great view of the mountains.

We went for a walk around the expansive hotel grounds and Teresa and the kids took the opportunity to go for a ride on a huge camel that happened to be there with his friendly master, and we spent the rest of the day at the swimming pool, splashing each other and enjoying the cooling of the day. That evening we ate a pleasant meal in the restaurant before retiring to bed for an early night. The kids went out like lights, even in those strange beds in that strange room. They do have their moments.

The next day, we ate a hearty breakfast (completely missing the real piggy bacon that was hidden around the corner at the hot buffet), played a game of mini-golf in remarkably hot morning conditions, and then headed back towards Dubai city.

Of course, we still had to do the weekly food shop, so we headed to Geant at Ibn Battuta and on the way out of the hypermarket I spotted a stand for a local hospital offering free health checks. The inner hypochondriac couldn't resist such attention, so I went and asked for a check, which was basically just a blood-pressure test. Surprise of surprises - it was pretty high. Over-complicated visa processes followed by food shopping with the kids? Well, duh.

Tuesday, October 31, 2006

Happy Hallowe'en...

As they say in many parts of the world. They even say it here now, although I don't know the Arabic for it. We even had some trick-or-treaters round tonight. I gave them some dates.

NOVEMBER

Saturday, November 04, 2006

Three months down...

How many to go? I don't know. Who knows what's round the next corner, other than time-travelling psychics with mirrors in their handbags?

So tomorrow, I will have been here three months. It's gone so quickly, but it feels like longer, if you know what I mean. Time plays tricks on the busy mind. So much has happened since I accepted the job whilst on holiday in Pembrokeshire back in July. That seems so distant now, in both miles and minutes.

And it could have been so different. During that week on holiday in Fishguard I also went for an interview for a job in Afghanistan, and it was pretty much there for the taking. The thing that made my mind up for me was the offer of free body armour. It clinched the decision to go to Dubai instead of a war zone.

But here we are, almost settled in; the weather is cooling all the time, making it a pleasure rather than a chore to take a walk outside. Eating out can be done on terraces and balconies now. We went for a bite at a "pub" called the Dhow and Anchor at the Jumeirah Beach Hotel the other night, sitting outside on the wooden decking amongst the twinkly-light-festooned palm trees and granite water features. We could see the towering form of the Burj Al Arab lurking just behind the trees, and we watched between mouthfuls of food as the lighting on the landward-side sail changing colour every few minutes from purple to blue; yellow to white. Shame the veal roast was a bit on the bland side.

So I ask myself: Does this sum it up? Is the place a triumph of style over substance? Do the glittering hotels and sparkling malls hide the reality? Is this city on the sand built on strong foundations, or are the movers and sheik-ers setting themselves up for a seriously big fall? Doubts crowd the mind, like over-concerned, fussy waiters who want to know if everything is alright with the meal. Does anyone ever answer in the negative? I don't, mainly because the staff have a knack of asking when you've got your mouth full. I only complain if it's really, really bad and completely inedible. This is, incidentally, why I'm banned from every branch of a certain chain restaurant where they wear Sunderland Shirts and herald the end of the working week.

I found an interesting link on another UAE blog the other day. It was to a short documentary on Youtube called Do Buy, and was made by a local director. It shows the sides of Dubai that you don't see reported in the glossy brochures or even in the papers that much. It's an eye opener for anyone in any doubt.

Personally speaking, it didn't take me too long to realise what was going on in Dubai. You can't help but notice the constant stream of wheezing white buses full of blue-overall-wearing, sullen-faced sub-con men being bussed from their labour camps to the many construction projects sprouting from the sand, where they invariably work twelve-hour days, six days a week, even in the insufferable height of summer. You can't help but notice the small armies of other blue-overall-wearing men that beaver away watering the grass or trimming the palm trees planted alongside the roads. Most of all, you can't help but notice that you don't see any of these people in the shopping malls.

The vast majority of the people in malls are Emiratis, Western expats, and professional family men from the Indian subcontinent who dress like Western expats. You don't see the labourers in there, or in the hotels, and yet these are the very men that built them. There's supposedly a ban on single men entering the malls at weekends, but I've been in them by myself many a time without being approached let alone asked to leave for wearing shocking shorts.

Being of a liberal, left-wing bias (I know, the shame), it is sometimes a strange feeling to live in a place that has been described by Jim Davidson as, "a right-winger's paradise," and he doesn't just mean that David Beckham likes the place. For once, the man is right. If you're rich here – or a Westerner at least – you will love it, because you can live an opulent lifestyle under constantly blue skies. What does that make me? A champagne friggin' socialist, no doubt. I prefer red wine anyway. It goes well with hypocrisy, I find.

And still, and still, what can you do? I *do* like it here, for the most part. I came here by choice; my eyes were wide open. I knew this place was an obscenely corpulent, ever-more-fattening capitalist's wet dream. Of course, I didn't know absolutely everything about it, and I still don't. I didn't know about the prostitution that is rife and completely brazen in areas of Bur Dubai, which came as something of a shock. I didn't know (despite the warnings) that driving here is akin to playing Russian roulette with an AK-47, with aggressive and dangerous driving that regularly takes the breath away, and almost daily encounters with the aftermath of another crash. This compels me to abandon even more of my tree-hugging principles, because when I get my visa sorted out I will probably buy a petrol-thirsty 4x4 or other large vehicle for the family. I just think they'll be safer in that than in a small family saloon. Am I wrong to want to protect my family?

Yes, my own hypocrisy does trouble me on occasion...well quite often, if I'm honest. I like the lifestyle. I like the sunshine. I like the mostly tax-free living. I understand that I'm a lucky sod for having what I have, even if I whine on and on about my health. I realise that I'm extremely fortunate to have been born where and when I was, with the best chance to live a more-than-comfortable life. I just have to close my eyes to it all, sometimes.

When I'm dodging speeding Prados and Landcruisers with permanently-flashing headlights and blacked-out windows on Sheik Zayed Road, I often see these dusty, white buses full of the blue overall brigade. I see them staring impassively at the illusory world outside, staring at us Western expats, our designer clothes and our expensive cars. I wonder what they are thinking. Are they envious? Are they angry at thinking they were buying a dream but being sold a nightmare by the callous, greedy labour agents? I'm sure they wouldn't want my pity. I'm just glad that I'm on this side of the window.

Tomorrow I fly to Doha for another look at the Big Hole in the Ground. I'm staying till Wednesday at least, so might not write for a while.

Thursday, November 09, 2006
Wherever you go in the world...

there are universal constants; undeniable truths that will never change.

The sun sets in the West.

Beer gets you drunk.

Quantity surveyors are boring.

And, most pertinent of all:

Hospital food is crap.

Anyway, it rained the other day. I missed it, because I didn't wake up in my private room in the hospitel (hospital/hotel) until it was gone. I opened the blinds to see strange, dark blotches on the car park tarmac which seemed to suggest that precipitation had occurred. The sky was white, misty and almost chilly-looking. Teresa confirmed that, yes indeed, it had rained that morning and it was, in fact, "that really fine stuff".

Oh, yeah. I was in the hospitel because last Sunday, the day after my last blog entry, the day I was meant to fly to Doha, I woke up to find I was having another episode of the dreaded atrial fibrillation. I thought about sitting it out and letting it go back in its own time – as I have done several times before - but since I was unsure of why it had happened this time (there's usually an identifiable trigger), I asked Teresa to drive me to the local health centre after she had dropped Joseph at school.

The doctor at the health centre tried to be reassuring. He carried out an ECG on me, and told me what I already knew - I was in AF. Between us we concluded that the new diet regime I started a few days ago might well have been the trigger this time. I'd been on a low-refined-carbohydrate diet (called the Paleo or Caveman diet) since the 1st November, which was four days prior to this episode.

Something didn't ring completely true to me, though. I was feeling quite good in myself up until Sunday night. I had got over the initial slight dizziness and my appetite was adjusting. More importantly, my ectopic beats (skipped beats that can be a precursor to AF) had reduced by a significant amount. I had actually had this diet recommended to me by someone on an internet message board for AF sufferers. Having had the condition for about six years, I was a regular reader of the board. What else could it have been, though: the ginger and lemon tea the night before, or the large diet Pepsi consumed at lunchtime the day before, maybe even the handful of walnuts eaten as an evening snack? I was confused.

The doctor decided to send me to see a cardiologist at a new hospital in the Bur Dubai area, near Port Rashid. We got directions and more reassurance, and with Teresa driving, we headed along the SZR towards the hospital. We landed and I booked into the ER. Another ECG was performed before I was transferred up to a small white, functional room in the Intensive Care/Cardio Care Unit. That may sound alarming, but they have the best equipment for dealing with matters of the heart.

Once I was settled in I suggested that Teresa should go home with Emma because Joseph needed to be picked up from school. After six years of this she knows the drill, and so do I, so she left me in the care of the hospital. I was soon covered in wires leading to sticky pads on my chest, wrists and ankles, and needles were stuck into various places on my hands and arms. I ended up with two IV drips this time, one in each hand.

They tried one drug on me, a beta-blocker, but it only slowed the fast rate down, so in the end they decided to put me under for a few minutes and zap me with the defibrillator. I've had it before, and it invariably works. The best bit is being gradually more drugged up with various legal substances, which make you feel like you've had a whole bottle of wine in thirty seconds, before the oxygen mask is placed over your face and they add the real knock-out stuff.

It was ever so slightly disconcerting to hear the nurse ask the anaesthetist if it was fifty millilitres, and the anaesthetist replying in a loud panicky voice that, no, it should be fifteen millilitres, just as they were injecting the sedatives. Before I knew it I was having a strange dream about being inside a computer or something, and then I was awake and back into blessed normal sinus rhythm.

It's hard to describe the feeling. It's mainly one of utter relief after being in AF and on edge for several hours. It's as if a huge - not agonising, but nagging - splinter has been removed from your bum. Lying there with AF is pretty crappy. People can tell me it isn't life-threatening in itself, etc., but when your heart is doing a dance like a drunken uncle doing the birdie-song, you constantly need to pee and you feel light-headed, it isn't very nice. Every time it happens I end up praying to God, and making deals with him about how I'll be good from now on, even though I'm a sworn agnostic with a leaning towards (without the utter certainty of) atheism. When it comes to these things, I'm not so much of a Pascal's Wager man as a big, girly coward.

After I was a bit more awake, I thanked the man who put me to sleep. He was a genial Libyan chap with an impossible name who had lived and worked in various UK locations for a good deal of his career. He melted back into the hospital hubbub as quickly as he had arrived, and I was left wondering what time I would be let out. Wishful thinking is what they call that.

The kind-eyed, touchy-feely cardiologist came and spoke to me and held my hand for what Westerners might consider to be an uncomfortably long time as he told me he wanted to keep me in ICU overnight, then transfer me down to ward for observation tomorrow. Blimey. In the UK, I've been pretty much sent home two hours after going back to NSR. The last time I'd had serious observations and tests was over two years ago when the AF had last reared its spitefully ugly face. Not this time, though. This doctor wanted to watch me and prod me and poke me, so who was I to argue? The only worry for me was the insurance. Would they cover it? Would I have to pay it and reclaim it? I rang Teresa and told her the good news. She was also surprised to hear that I was staying in overnight.

So I spent that night in that small white room with no TV and nothing to read. I did get some food, and it was pretty good, but then all food tastes great when you've not been allowed to eat for hours. I didn't get much sleep. The automatic blood pressure monitor inflated every hour through the night and then the nurses came to take more blood every six hours. Then there were the blood-thinning injections into my belly. Along with all those wires and tubes, I defy anyone to sleep well under such conditions. They should think about using it at Guantanamo Bay as a new form of torture. I was ready for some more of that magic bottle of wine in a syringe from The Affable Sandman of Tripoli.

The next morning I rang Teresa and the boss and told them the score. I was going down to the ward and was likely to spend at least another night there. Finally they released me from the drips and monitor wires and I performed a very unsteady stand-up routine that wasn't very funny at all, and managed to walk around for a bit. They wheel-chaired me down to the ward, and I was in for a bit of a surprise. Being used to the good ole' British National Health Service, I expected a large public ward with peeling walls, full of coughing old men in ill-fitting pyjamas surrounded by bored relatives. But of course, all health care is private here, and I got my own private hotel-style room, with a separate lounge, a TV in each room, a wardrobe and an empty fridge. A mini-bar might have been too much to expect, in hindsight.

As time wore on I ate increasingly poor specially-prepared low-fat food, drank water and watched The Golden Girls on TV. The family came and went, soon growing bored of seeing Daddy plodding around the room in an open-backed gown. The vital sign checks and blood pressure tests carried on at four-hourly intervals, but just before bedtime (well, you're always in a bed in hospital) the nurses noticed my blood pressure was up a bit. They took it again to check about half an hour later and it was down a bit. The next morning, as I waited for the doc to come and discharge me, they took my BP again, and it was high again. They started getting a bit more urgent about it, bringing doctors in, and another two checks later, they were asking me about hypertension and family medical history and all kinds of things. Hmm. Me - Hypertensive? Don't be so bloody stupid! I've already moved past 'H' in the medical dictionary.

I was given a really nasty-tasting dissolving tablet to stick under my tongue and promptly wheeled down to the Cardio Outpatient clinic where they performed an ultrasound scan of my ticker. After ten minutes of having a gelled-up device slid all over my chest, the doctor told me that I was definitely suffering from hypertension and my heart was showing signs of it that indicated a long-term problem, maybe going back three or more years. It had avoided detection until now.

He told me that the high BP was making my heart work harder, and it was now over-muscled, like some mad keen body-builder. The problem with big muscles is that they get stiff and eventually weaken. Oh bugger. At the same time, as it dawned on me, the doc was telling me that the hypertension could be the major factor behind my AF. It's not often you are happy to find out you've got a condition, but this time I was, because if it's true, I have found out what has caused all this crap I've been putting up with for the last six years. Now I could treat it. Now, just maybe, I could beat it.

I knew what was coming next. The doctor told me I had to stay another night. He told me I had to go on medication. He told me to go on a diet. He told me to exercise! The list of drugs I was on was growing: anti-arrhythmic, anti-cholesterol, anti-aircraft, anti-anuncle and now anti-high blood pressure.

It's kind of at odds with what I'm trying to achieve with this Paleo diet, because they are yet to dig up the remains of a *Homo erectus* branch of Boots the Chemist from a hundred thousand years back. I really want to be drug free and not have to remember to take three or four different pills at various times of the day. C'est la vie. Well, my vie, anyway.

I went back to the ward with a strange sense of elation mixed with terror. Now I know what has to be done. If I do it right, and lose the requisite weight and lower my cholesterol and blood pressure, I should be able to get off the meds within a year or two, one by one. I know that from now on I hold my destiny, or at least a great deal of it, in my own hands. I have been given control.

I finally left hospital yesterday, and was just glad to get away in the end. The hotel-style room had impressed me to start with, but after two days in there, I was bouncing off the walls. The TV was my only companion for much of the time, and it was starting to grate with its repeats of Roseanne and Different Strokes and straight-to-video movies.

The doc gave me a final pep talk and told me that while nothing was outright banned now, I had to remember the simple golden rule: the more legs an animal has, the worse it is for you. It's like Orwell's Animal Farm in reverse: four legs bad, two legs good, no legs even better. I hope he means fish, not snakes. I did wonder if this was a case for cannibalism, although I wouldn't eat myself given the choice; far too fatty.

It's kind of fitting that this has happened now. I came to Dubai for a new beginning, a new life, and all that guff. I was worried about my health, naturally, but carried on as normal, if not worse than I used to if I'm honest, eating and drinking crap and living the lazy, luxury, expat lifestyle. My weight got to its highest ever, and my stress levels also got higher, for one reason and another. I now realise that stress has been a factor all along, and along with the obesity, it is a potent combination.

I did have a really bad stress-out session the day before my latest episode. That probably helped to send my BP through the roof and kick the AF off. I'd even had that warning at the shopping mall just a few days ago. But every cloud has a silver lining. The thoroughness of the medical care here has impressed me, especially my cardiologist, who has been encouraging and reassuring and also frank with me about where I am. I now have a positive outlook, and feel ready to put right the years of abuse my body has suffered. I have gone right off fatty and sugary foods. I'm not a puddingy person any more, as my dear Mother says.

The insurance wasn't a problem. I showed my company insurance card, signed a couple of forms and didn't have to pay a penny. Emergency care is free!

Sunday, November 12, 2006
Doha or bust...

I get the feeling Doha doesn't want me to enjoy its charms again. The week after *Eid* I was meant to go and talk about the Big Hole in the Ground, but I couldn't find a hotel room for love nor money or even saucy shenanigans in the scullery, so I had to call it all off. Then last week, I managed to find a hotel room booked, but ended up in the much-vaunted hospitel, so again the trip was off.

Today, back at work, the owners of the Big Hole in the Ground are still insistent that I should go to Doha for a few days. Well, fine, but let me find a hotel room, or find one for me. OK, said they. I spent most of the day chasing various people hither and thither by phone and e-mail, and I finally managed to get hold of a lady who was supposed to help, and it transpires that I might actually have a room, but it isn't a hundred percent certain, and the room in question is really expensive. I'm not paying for it, so that last problem isn't really mine. There's the small matter of the Asian Games approaching, you see, and as a result hotel rooms are rarer than rocking horse faeces. Rumour Central would have use believe that the place isn't even ready to hold the games. They say it about everywhere where they hold one of these big events. People just like to whinge. Don't I, dear?

But anyway, I am undeterred. Tomorrow I'm getting on that plane for the short (but still potentially terrifying) hop to Doha. Even if I end up kipping in a bus shelter, I've got to be there and do my stuff. I've even changed my hospital appointment with the cardiologist so I can go. Committed? I should be.

I think an important lesson today was (again) not to sweat the small stuff. I get stressed out about things far too easily, and it has to be affecting my blood pressure. A friend told me today that the frustration of living here with all the traffic and the bureaucracy and the regular use of the word *Insha'allah* (literal translation: God willing; actual meaning: I am not taking responsibility) was understandable.

He also said that some people are just more stressed than others, and for the stressed among us, being told to calm down is the worst thing they can hear. I wholeheartedly agree with that sentiment, as my family will tell you.

But then, if it's my nature or not, I need to control it or focus it or something. I need to laugh more and find a creative outlet. And I should stop supporting Middlesbrough Football Club.

Friday, November 17, 2006

Things to do in Doha when you're ...

bored and lonely, don't know the city and don't have a car:

A) Visit the Pearl Lounge bar attached to the side of the Marriott hotel. There you will be made to feel completely unwelcome, and on entry will be keenly quizzed as to your room number and name like you're a criminal suspect before being hastily ushered to the bar because all the tables are reserved even though the place is emptier than Paris Hilton's head. Even when you manage to convince them to let you sit at a table by telling them you won't be staying long, they watch you like hawks wearing bi-focals as you slide down the friction-free, leather-clad bucket seats, toying with your over-iced Jamesons and wondering what kind of people come to a place like this, apart from lonely and bored businessmen, of course. The lighting is non-existent, so much so, that the drinks menus have little torches attached to them. There are large Plasma screen TVs dotted around the walls, showing scenes of snowy mountains and trendy people skiing down them on a permanent loop, all accompanied by instantly forgettable chill/trance/techno-pap. You should probably have more than one drink, just to annoy them, and see if anyone comes in. When people do appear, they look at you like you are sitting there in the altogether. Finally, when you've had enough of feeling as welcome as Timothy Mallett at a wake, the bill appears in your face and you leave, tutting to yourself about the utter absurdity of it all, and swearing never to go that kind of place again. Until next time you're alone and bored in a strange city. Still, you feel slightly amused and smug as a couple of Japanese businessmen (dressed smartly enough) try to get in as you're leaving and get turned away from an almost-empty club because they aren't hotel guests.

B) Lie on the hotel bed in your pants eating chocolate and watching TV.

It's a shame that I chose A, really, because the trip was otherwise a reasonably good experience. Well, OK, the plane was an hour late, and there were no taxis to be had when I landed, which meant a thirty minute wait for one to take me half a mile along the road to my firm's local office. I know: I should have walked.

After a short visit to the office I had a really interesting experience in the most banged-up, crappy car I've ever been in, because there still weren't any taxis to be had, and the office admin/gopher chap (an insanely friendly Sudanese fellow called Jamal) had to give me a lift to my next destination. It's possible that the giant Ory the Oryx on the Corniche had eaten all the taxis, but anyway, this car was a wreck, and that's being disrespectful to wrecks. The headlights were smashed in and the wing mirrors hung off, and the rust was just about holding it together. I even had to push it to get it going, and jumped in as it spluttered and coughed into life.

Jamal was quite a good driver, but with my seat set at a permanent forty-five-degree recline and no seat belt available, I didn't feel very safe. When we inevitably encountered a Qatari in a white 4x4 who cut across us, Jamal spat out a stream of exotic-sounding expletives and gesticulated wildly at the other driver. Getting to the hotel was a relief.

The hotel itself was a smooth operation and they were falling over themselves to help me at every turn. Every corner I turned seemed to reveal another oriental person in bell-boy get-up greeting me with the now-familiar American-accented, nasal whine of, "Good Morning, Sir," or something similar. The restaurants had good food and excellent service. The room was pleasant, and the free use of the business lounge (with four free alcoholic drinks a night) was a nishe touch. Oh yesh, oshifer. What big handcuffsh you have...

The primary aims of the trip were achieved as well. We had loads of meetings about the Big Hole in the Ground, discussing how much it was going to cost to actually build something in the hole and how long it was going to take, etc., and in the end people were satisfied with what I did, or at least I think they were.

On my second night a few of the people involved in the project went for dinner in a nice Italian in the Rydges Plaza hotel, and as if by magic, the conversation turned to politics. We had a Brit (me), a South African, and Australian, an Iraqi and two Palestinians (one Christian, one Muslim) around the table, and it was the tactful Australian who broke the shop talk up spectacularly with a question about the whereabouts of a certain Mr. Bin Laden. Some strong (and surprising) viewpoints were offered, but everyone managed to come away smiling and still on talking terms. The consensus was that the British had managed to fuck up the Middle East after both World wars, and now the Americans were carrying on where we had left off. Scars run deep round here, it seems.

Apart from everything else, I found myself thinking how lucky I am to be living in Dubai. Doha is trying desperately to catch up with Dubai, but the general feeling around here is that they are about ten to fifteen years behind, at least. There aren't as many things for tourists and expats to do, and the infrastructure is quite poor. People who work here constantly tell me they wish they didn't. Some even fly to Dubai every weekend. On the other hand, I bet they don't spend as much money living in Doha.

The Asian games that start in December are looming large now. It's quite obvious that Doha is going to struggle, because hotel rooms are just impossible to get now, and traffic is getting heavier and heavier while they attempt to finish all the new roads and tart up the airport, finish the unfinished roads and erect huge scaffolding structures covered in plywood to carry advertising for the games. Surely everyone here knows what's happening, anyway.

The taxi situation stinks. It appears that they are all being used to transport officials and dignitaries all over the place these days, although I have been secretly hoping that it was really the giant oryx that had devoured them. There are no viable alternatives to the motor car here, because public transport is even worse here than it is in Dubai, and that's saying something. Even so, I hope they pull it off and show the continent a good time. I hope the games give the place a good kick-start towards catching up with its bigger, glitzier neighbour.

I eventually left Doha after four days, looking forward to seeing my wife and kids again. The week had gone a lot quicker than the previous one that I had spent in hospital, that's for sure. The plane out of Doha was forty minutes late in departing, and I spent the whole flight quietly fuming as men in Arab national dress spent the flight sending text messages from their mobiles, despite the many in-your-face reminders to turn off all such equipment.

I try to be understanding of cultural differences, but this annoyed me. They knew they were doing wrong, because they hid their phones when any cabin crew passed close. Some - I stress *some* - of these people just don't appear to give a fig about rules, regulations, common courtesy and cultural norms and believe themselves to be invincible and above everyone else because they wear a dish-dash. It's a shame, because a few bad eggs end up giving everyone else a bad name. My biggest worry is that I'm in danger of becoming the kind of person I hate...a racist bigot who tars everyone with the same nasty brush. I've heard it said more than once that it happens to some people.

Despite all this, and despite some of the strangest and most worrying mechanical noises I've ever heard on an aeroplane, we landed safely. I am getting better at flying, and I guess I don't have a choice but to do so with all the flying that is done round here. My fear levels are reducing every time, but I still have my little superstitions and routines that I have to go through: I always read the safety information card on both sides; I invariably end up praying to that God who must be seriously pissed off with hearing from this agnostic again, and I always find my imagination running riot with the infinite number of ways a plane can come to harm on the ground and in the air as we taxi out to the runway. Statistics can say what they want, but there's just something unnatural about hurtling at just shy of the speed of sound in a pressurised metal tube six miles up in the air. It's a wonder I manage to keep myself from screeching like a little girl when my thoughts run away with themselves like this.

It took me just an hour to pass through Dubai airport this time. Passport control was a chew as ever, with long queues for non-residents, and it will continue to be a chew until my company get my residence visa sorted out. I remembered to pick up some duty free alcohol this time, though, so it eased some of the earlier frustrations. Until I get my residence visa, I can't get my alcohol licence, and can't buy any liquor from the official alcohol outlets outside the airport to have at home. In fact, the laws being the way they are here, I was probably breaking the law by taking the booze home with me, even though I was allowed to buy it in Duty Free. What was I supposed to do: stand there and guzzle all the bottles down before I left the airport?

Anyway, I managed to find a taxi quite quickly, as you would reasonably expect at an international airport, and within an hour I was home, and my kids ran with outstretched arms to greet the bags of goodies I'd brought them. It's good to be home again.

Sunday, November 19, 2006
Nothing Gets In The Way Of Ssergorp...

Nothing, you hear?

So, if the powers-that-be decide to stop the unrestricted internet access available in the Dubai Internet City areas and subject it to Etisalat and their poxy proxy and its inherent censorship, that's Ssergorp.

And if they decide that they're going to introduce a trial road toll system next year on the Sheik Zayed and Garhoud Bridge Roads, even though the alternative routes aren't very good and there will be no Metro in place until 2009 at least, that's real Ssergorp.

And, if they decide that they won't renew the fifteen percent rent increase cap (for what it was worth), thus giving landlords huge boners all across the land, that's Ssergorp again, even if we beg the Great God of Market Forces to bring about the Great Blessed Correction.

Best of all, though, if the company you work for pays you on random days by cheques which take forty-eight hours to clear rather than by good old-fashioned electronic transfer, and they take over three and a half months to get you a residence visa, that's definitely Ssergorp.

However, if the powers-that-be decide that the stout fellows who work all hours in crappy conditions and live in ever crappier conditions should have some rights and protection and some health insurance, etc., well that is PROGRESS, and should be applauded.

It's just a shame that it seems to be a case of one step forward and three steps back.

I shall stop whining now and get on with living the dream.

Monday, November 27, 2006

Christmas is coming...

The camel is looking bemused. I think it's their default expression.

In this peculiarly unique place, the clashes of cultures still have the power to amaze, amuse and completely bamboozle. I took a walk through the shopping mall they call Wafi City the other day, a kind of loosely Egyptian-styled, sand-coloured monolith with stained-glass pyramids perched on top. Inside, high-fashion and high-tech shops mingle with high-fat fast food franchise outlets...which I avoid now, of course in my quest to become Brad Pitt...with a receding hairline.

But the mall has now become a Christmas wonderland. Slap-bang in the middle of the central plaza, underneath one of the pyramids, is a giant Christmas tree, adorned with shiny baubles and twinkling lights. Around the bottom of the tree there are some white hoardings, with the words "ELVES AT WORK" painted on it in various places. It seems that there will be a grotto at the bottom of the tree, and they're going to have a big light-switching-on ceremony on Thursday, according to an information board. Dotted around other parts of the mall are other Christmas displays, such as small cottages with snow-covered roofs and pairs of red-suited, black-booted legs sticking out of the chimney.

It jars the senses seeing all this. Firstly, it's thirty degrees centigrade and sunny outside. Secondly, this is a Muslim country. I've been in non-Christian countries around Christmas before, and knew that there would probably be a few trees here and there, and shops selling Christmassy stuff for the large Western expat population, but I never thought I'd see a mall in the Middle East trying to outdo the Metro Centre for sheer festive cheese overload.

It's confusing, really, because even here I get told that Christmas is being banned in the UK because of politically-correct do-gooders, etc., but here we are looking at a forty-foot-high symbol of a Christian festival, and the dish-dash-wearing men and their *abbaya*-adorned wives don't bat an eyelid. You have to wonder what UK tabloids like the Sun or the Daily Mail would make of some Ramadan decorations being put up in the Trafford Centre. Probably best not to think about it, to be honest.

Then I think...does this show Christmas up for what it really is today? It isn't much of a religious festival nowadays, if we're honest.

All the paraphernalia in the malls are based around trees, lights, baubles, snowy scenes, stockings, candy canes, toys, presents, and consumerism gone mad. In that respect, it fits Dubai like a glove. More chances to spend, spend, spend. You can buy nativity scenes in the shops if you so wish, but there doesn't seem to be much of a market for them. I think it's probably fair to say that this is the case in the UK as well. The religious aspect of Christmas is a side-show to most people, and maybe that's why it's so easily accepted and assimilated around the world now, because it can almost be celebrated without mentioning Jesus at all.

Christmas: It's only four weeks away now. It just doesn't feel right. We went to the beach at the Jumeirah Beach Park on Saturday, and enjoyed the warm sunshine, yellow sand and clear Gulf waters, although even here, in a pay-to-enter beach, it was still full of fag-ends and other rubbish. We have promised the kids a visit to Ski Dubai before or around Christmas, and we'll have a snowball fight and do some sledging, then maybe have some fondue and mulled wine in the alpine-styled restaurant afterwards. On Christmas Day itself we are planning to have dinner in a hotel or at a golf club. We will obviously miss our families, but with their visits due to start in February, it won't be too bad. Whatever happens, our first Christmas in a warm country will be an adventure.

That reminds me, we need to go and buy a tree...I see they have them in IKEA. AARRGGHH!!!!

Wednesday, November 22, 2006
Fitness Freaky

I've always thought of gyms as places of torture where sado-masochists go for their fix of watching other, more muscled people admiring themselves in the mirror. Now I am joining their ranks.

Tonight I went to a gym and tortured myself for over an hour with exercise bikes and various resistance machines that wouldn't look out of place in a medieval dungeon. The Inquisition boys would have loved this place.

As it happens, the things I hate most about gymnasiums - other people, who are generally healthier, better-looking, more muscled, you get picture - weren't there. I had the place ALL to myself. Now this is because it's a fairly small gym at the top of a hotel. Hotel gyms aren't very busy at any time, so I'm well in here. It's got a pool and a jacuzzi and a steam room and a sauna and really very plush facilities in the changing room, with brilliant white bowl-style sinks and frosted glass on all the doors and little up-lighters on the walls. Ooh, I've come over all Lawrence Llewynn-Bowen. All the equipment is brand new and the cardio machines have little TVs that can be toggled on and off with the exercise data, or even shared on a split screen with it. Cool.

The reason I'm going to this particular gym is that I won a month's free membership by answering a few questions on a radio phone-in quiz a few weeks back. I also won a meal and a night in the hotel for two, which is nice. The presenters, Cat Boy and Geordie Bird on Dubai 92, gave me pretty easy questions, to be fiar. When he asked me what I did (not as in that dreadful "and what do you do?" style you hear at stuck-up dinner parties) I told him I was a quantity surveyor. He sounded suitably impressed and said I must be intelligent. As I said to Cat Boy: it's not exactly brain science.

Anyway, the good thing about the prize is that it's given me a reason to go along and start off the exercising phase of my new healthy lifestyle. Stop laughing at the back. I've been sticking to my eating plan, which is a sort of modified paleo diet. I don't eat very much bread, pasta or potatoes, and if I do, it's the wholemeal stuff. Most of the food I eat is lean poultry and fish, vegetables, rice, oats, fruit and nuts.

I've even found myself going off junk food. Even when we went to the Johnny Rockets burger joint (a fabulously kitsch stainless-steel-plated, 1950s-style American diner) last week, I thought about treating myself to a burger, but went for the chicken club on brown bread instead (easy on the mayo), and it was very tasty. I couldn't even face more than two of Teresa's chips. They just tasted greasy and bland.

So far, I've lost seven kilograms, or maybe more, because I didn't start weighing myself immediately. That's fifteen pounds or just over one stone for any imperialists out there. I seem to have switched over quite easily to this way of thinking, and I put it down to what happened to me a couple of weeks ago with my visit to hospital. I've never felt so motivated to do it and have never felt so sure that I can do it. I've even got a cold, which always seems to happen within four weeks of starting these regimes, but I'm nearly over it, fingers crossed, and I can put proper effort it.

The first gym session was hard work. The Indian personal trainer man (who was small but strong, as he showed when demonstrating machines) was a great help and showed me how to use everything, and even took me through a slightly shortened general workout with cardio and resistance training. He counted my reps and gently encouraged me to do the leg extensions, shoulder presses and hyperextensions (not hypertensions).

After I finished and had my shower, I felt like I was walking on air. I had a real buzz. The only little annoyance was a bit of acid reflux during and after the session, but I put that down to the very acidic cough sweets I've been taking for my cough. I drove home, hearing the superb new U2 song on the radio on the way, and had some grilled fish and veg for me tea. I am in danger of becoming a bit of a health bore with all this, but if I keep the right mindset going, I don't really care. I'm sick of being sick.

Wednesday, November 29, 2006
Clerical and Medical

What a bloody palaver that was. Excuse the language, but *bugger me!*

The fact that it has taken four months to get to this point is neither here nor there, but I finally went to have my medical today, which is the compulsory blood test and chest X-ray everyone coming to work in Dubai has to go through. They test you for HIV and TB, and if you have either, you are summarily deported. If you're clear, you can have a visa and get on with living the dream, *habibi*.

Being a worrier, I wonder if there's the slightest chance that I could have got HIV from somewhere, even though I know I haven't exposed myself to the risks (honest, m'lud). I mean, I *really* am a worrier. Even if the odds are billions to one against something occurring, it will not matter, especially if it's something really, really bad that I can play over and over in my mind, such as a plane crashing, an asteroid hitting the planet, or a black hole swallowing up the contents of my sock drawer.

But anyway: the test. It was performed out at the Maktoum hospital (this name is everywhere, do they own the place or something?) which is in Deira, which is itself on the other side of the creek. I was told by the HR manager to go early – before 7.30am ideally – so as to avoid queuing for several weeks. I was also advised to park at work, i.e. just this side of the creek, and catch a taxi there and back. My advisors told me that this would only take an hour or so. Who was I to doubt this advice?

I drove to work, parked in the office multi-storey car park and managed to hail down a cab within a minute; so far so good. We crossed Garhoud Bridge without a problem, but the traffic in Deira was a mess; vehicles of all shapes and sizes crept at the speed of snails riding on tortoises' backs along the roads, blocking up all the junctions and roundabouts. The drivers amused themselves with some kind of free-form jazz played on car horns, which provided a constant staccato of noise in the air all around. Asian and Arab men gesticulated at each other, and I shook my head. I have come to learn that banging it off stuff is generally more painful.

We had been stuck on one roundabout for nearly ten minutes when the driver cheerily announced that the hospital was just round the corner, so I sighed loudly, threw some notes at him, and walked the rest of the way. It was 7.35am.

I walked through the hospital gates and thanked *Allah* that I was a privileged Westerner with private health cover. The Maktoum hospital is grim, let's just leave it at that. I quickly found the Admin office (this is gonna be a cinch, I remember thinking) and promptly entered through the Female entrance. They sent me packing, even though I offered to show my (now-reducing) man-boobs as evidence. I re-entered through the Male waiting area and sat down on a creaky chair. Five minutes later I had handed over my documents, paid my money and was in possession of my Government health card and a slip of paper. This would allow me to procure the requisite tests, but it had to be typed up in the Typing Office first.

Then it really started turning fruit-formed. Without any directions offered or signs in sight it took me an age to find the Typing Office. It was in a pre-fabricated hut hidden round the back of some other tatty building. When I eventually found it I was told by the man who was sat there doing not very much - other than drinking coffee and picking fluff out of his navel - that it would take fifteen minutes. To give him his due, it took him only eight minutes and twenty-four seconds, and then I was handed another piece of paper. Go back to the Admin office, was the blunt, disinterested order, so I trudged back round there and paid some more money and received the proper typed-up slip for the tests. Now go to the testing room, was the instruction. Er...where's that? The response was a grunt and a nonchalant wave in a vague direction. Oh, this *is* fun.

After another ten minutes of fruitless searching I found the X-ray department, but I *had* to go for the blood test first, so they told me to follow the green line backwards to the blood test laboratory which was over near the side entrance. Well, it could have been the main entrance. I really don't know, and by then, I really didn't care.

I entered the Male section this time and was greeted with a large room full of chairs set out in rows like church pews and four windowed hatches at the far end. Above the hatches was an electronic display board, showing a group of three-digit numbers that flashed and changed at random intervals. It all looked like some Argos / mental home hybrid that I dreamed about once. I shuffled glumly towards the windows, not having a clue which one to go to, but a kindly young chap with a mischievous smile who was already waiting told me which window to go to. I handed over my papers and was directed to sit down.

My papers then moved from the first window across to the last one, in some kind of process that had me wondering what was for tea tonight. Then a large group of sub-continental labourer types entered the room and sat together in a tight, protective huddle at the other side of the room, like penguins in an Arctic (or is it Antarctic?) gale. A man who was apparently escorting the labourers dumped all their papers at the *last* window, and then all their numbered tickets started appearing as if by magic. I think this annoyed the mischievous young man and his mates. He went to the windows and spoke in rapid-fire Arabic. "How come they got to push in?" was the general gist of it, I would imagine.

Time was dragging on. I resigned myself to waiting a long time. So much for the early start, I thought. But out of the blue, my name was called and I got my numbered ticket. I was number 327, not a free man. I sat down again, and five minutes later the numbers on the board changed about a dozen times, bleeping manically each time, before settling on a group of numbers ending in 327. I followed the herd to a smaller waiting area with about ten chairs in it, sitting amongst Indian and Pakistani men of different shapes and sizes. They watched me impassively but with a definite air of suspicion. The moment they got the chance, they all moved away from me into vacated seats, flocking together in their little group again. I lifted my arm and sniffed my armpit loudly.

Presently my number was barked from the next room, and I entered a veritable factory of blood testing. There were maybe a dozen of what looked like decommissioned electric chairs in there with various doctors and nurses sat next to them, waiting to take our blood, so I sat down at the nearest free one. As the doctor stuck the cold steel into my vein he made some small talk about where I was from and what my favourite breed of cow was. I barely felt the needle. With my medical history I've become so used to the whole process that I could probably do it myself.

Then, with a plaster holding a lump of cotton wool over the hole in the crook of my elbow, I followed the green line back to the X-ray department, where there were yet more windows and seats. I handed more documents over, and was soon doing a contortionist act against the X-ray screen to get my chest flat against it. And that was it.

Not too bad, I thought, but when I checked my watch I realised it was just after 9.15am. What a kerfuffle. All these administrative tasks could be done in one place, yet they choose to separate them into the smallest components and make something that should be simple really quite complex. Is it to give people jobs? It must cost a fortune.

Mission accomplished, I headed out of the hospital and started the search for a taxi to take me back over the creek and to the office. This part proved to be the worst bit of the whole experience. Being a man of short patience, I didn't do what I should have done, i.e. waited for a taxi to drop someone off at the hospital. No, instead I wandered out towards the main roads, thinking my chances would be better there. As it was, I saw dozens of taxis, but they were almost all occupied. I saw maybe three unoccupied cars, but they zoomed past, ignoring my increasingly desperate waving and shouting.

I ended up walking all the way to the creek, well the road alongside and near where we parked after brunch at the Hyatt. I don't know how far I walked in all, but it was over a mile, I'm sure of it. Eventually a taxi dropped someone off at a large office building and I leapt into it, relieved, hot, sweaty and completely stressed out, as is my wont. I just couldn't believe that it had been so difficult to find a taxi in a place as busy as Deira. Lesson for today: stay put.

I expected the drive back over the creek to be horrendous, but it wasn't. It took less than twenty minutes, and I got back to the office at around 10.30am. I was glad to get that over with. This is one of the last steps towards getting my full visa. If everything is OK, I will have it within ten days to two weeks, fingers crossed...*Insha'allah*. It has been a frustrating first four months in the sense that I haven't been able to establish myself fully with my own car, proper banking facilities, a liquor licence, etc. It looks like we're finally getting there.

DECEMBER

Saturday, December 02, 2006

Rain, Rain, Rain and even more rain.

It's been pissing it down all day; hasn't stopped. It rained quite a bit yesterday and last night as well. Driving along the roads here is now even more interesting than it usually is, with huge puddles - nay *rivers* - where the inadequate drainage is failing to clear the surface water. In the puddles there are soapy bubbles. Apparently, they put detergent on the road before it rains to prevent the many oil slicks from turning into ice rinks.

As a result we've been stuck indoors all weekend. We went to the cinema at the Ibn Battuta mall yesterday, taking Emma to see her first ever proper movie. She didn't watch much of the film and wouldn't sit on her seat, but she was fine. We managed to keep her close to us by showing her the popcorn every so often. Then we had tea at Tony Roma's. They have a branch in Taiwan which I had a few incredibly calorific meals in, mainly due to the amazing pork ribs they serve, especially the baby back variety. However, here in Arabia, as you may have gathered, pork is only available in certain places, and Tony Roma's, who are famous for ribs, is not one of those places. They only do one type of rib here: beef. That's by the by. I still had a half portion - no fries - and they were OK, but the service was terrible. They got most of the orders wrong and the food was lukewarm.

Never mind. Today we went to the Mall of the Emirates and had a spot of lunch in Apres, a sort of alpine-style, *après-ski* place with fondues on the menu, and a large window taking up the whole of one end of the room showing people falling over on the ski slopes of Ski Dubai. It was very pleasant, of course, even though Emma managed to knock over two glasses of wine, meaning I only managed to drink one in the end. I don't think she did it on purpose.

On the way home in the continuing rain I saw a sight I have seen too much of since coming here. I saw a car going along the road with young kids in the back, jumping around, completely unrestrained. It was a Western family as well. I found myself wondering just what the *hell* these morons are thinking. Is it really such a pain in the arse to strap your kids in safely? Would they do it in the UK? No, I bet, so why do it here, where the chances of an accident are so much higher? The sheer selfish stupidity of it just amazes me. Have they become so spoilt and lazy by living a luxury lifestyle that they can't be bothered to do anything that takes the slightest effort? Do they not know what can happen to a loose child in a crash? I know locals do it as well, but they could have some tenuous claim to ignorance and cultural something or other...well, they probably can't...but it still shocks me to see people doing it when they should know better.

Taking a deep breath, counting to ten...and end preaching.

Wednesday, December 06, 2006
The sands of time...

slither grain by grain, inexorably towards an unknown future. With every second that passes, another life is made, another life ends. Somewhere around this rock floating in infinite, inky darkness, someone falls in love. Somewhere in Dubai, my puny skills prove to be no match for the DARK SIDE OF THE FORCE.

Ahem. Where were we? Well, I'm still waiting for my residence visa. I found out today that I haven't got HIV, which is nice. Now I only worry about black holes and comets.

At least work has been interesting. I've been working like a dog - pronounced *dawg*, obviously - a dog in a suit and tie, in an office at a computer, which isn't really what a dog does, to be honest, but for further info please talk to my psychotherapist. And yet my company, who shall remain nameless, still haven't paid me for the month of November. They keep putting me off and saying the equivalent of "the cheque is in the post".

I also found out I have to fork out a load of money to sponsor my family. This *isn't* nice, especially with Christmas just round the corner; approaching like a white Land Cruiser with the obligatory heavily-tinted windows on the SZR, headlights flashing manically. So I'm slightly peeved, if truth be told, and starting to go a little crazy, to boot. You may have noticed.

The administration in my company is somewhat erratic. I don't understand why we can't be paid by automatic electronic transfer on a set date every month instead of being at the mercy of senior management's unpredictable movements and certain planetary alignments in order to get the requisite two signatures on every pigging cheque.

The atmosphere at work has gone downhill of late. Paying us late doesn't help, but in addition, we've all been told that we *must* wear ties at all times. Mine gets wet in the shower, but it doesn't wash with the boss. Everyone's up to their eyeballs and panicking and snappy and grumpy and when a few of us sit together for lunch, we invariably moan about work, with the management and the administration team getting much of the criticism.

They haven't even announced a Christmas Party. Maybe it's been cancelled this year. Maybe I'll turn into Tiny Tim. The sad thing is, for me anyway, a happy ship is a productive ship whilst an unhappy ship loses its deck-swabbers and its cabin boys like that (clicks fingers). I've lost count of the number of times people have said that they're going to quit. It's not as if there's a shortage of work round here. If you don't like it leave, right? Wrong. The company and its local sponsors own us and if they feel that way inclined or don't want us working for another company in Dubai they can just refuse to give us a Letter of No Objection, which means we are effectively banned from taking another job for two years.

Anyway......

I'd better be careful. The ears have walls and the eyes have hills, etc. At least I ain't writing this at work.

Waiver: The opinions stated in this are a load of old bollocks. Names have been changed (and not even mentioned) to protect the guilty. The writer is a highly-strung muppet with a penchant for self-pity and self-righteous bluster. Please send cash now.

At least I'm still doing the gym thing. I'm going every night of the week, and Teresa and Joseph are not really happy, because it means I don't get home till after 8.30 or 9.00pm. The thing is, the hotel is just off the SZR, which means it is best to go straight there from work, rather than going home first then driving back the wrong way (with all the traffic heading back to Deira/Sharjah, etc.) because even at 8 or 9pm, the traffic is still a complete bleeding nightmare. I have tried it once or twice, and a fifteen-minute journey can take up to an hour going that way. I've decided that when my free membership is finished, I'll join the gym here in Springs. Then I can come home, see the kiddies and then go to the gym to get all sweaty.

I had a good session tonight, as it happens, even though I hadn't felt particularly keen on going. After taking a long lunch (much to the boss's displeasure) and having a long walk around the Cityscape Exhibition at the Exhibition Centre I was fairly tired. The trade fair was enormous, with models of buildings and developments that looked amazing and ridiculously ambitious. The local developer who is our client for the job in Doha had their own stand and there was an eight-foot high model of the building that is eventually supposed to emerge from the Big Hole in the Ground. It'll be nice when it's finished...as everyone says round these parts.

Crikey, it was a month ago that I went into hospital with my last AF episode! The time has just sped by, and with the new drugs and eating regime and the exercise I am feeling so much better, and my heart flutters (which used to be frequent) have quietened right down. Long may it continue. My goal is to be drug free, healthy and my ideal weight in a year's time. Oh, and rich and famous would be nice too.

Tuesday, December 12, 2006
BUGGER ME...

I got my residence visa today!

It only took five and a half months.

Saturday, December 16, 2006
Deeper and deeper

I finally got my residence visa last week. It happened surprisingly considering the medical results have only just come through. It means I can do things like buy a car and means I don't have to leave the country every two months. I've also got my UAE driving licence, after another visit to yet another red-tape nightmare (police station this time) with more multiple points of liaison and more sitting waiting for your number to be called while other people ignore the queuing system and just wander up to the counter, sometimes even interrupting when other people are being dealt with.

It probably wouldn't have been half as bad if I had actually had my original passport with me, even though I'd been told by the HR manager that I didn't *need* the original. As it was, I had to drive all the way to work to collect my passport through atrocious weather (the wettest December in eleven years, we are told) and trying to get back without getting stuck in a traffic jam on SZR caused by an awful accident early that morning, which I later found out claimed nine souls. It seems that people were driving too fast for the conditions. Again.

After getting back to the police station and waiting some more, I eventually walked away with a nice new shiny gold credit-card-sized licence. I also got a nice parking ticket to go with it. Hurrah!

Traffic, traffic, traffic. It's really starting to grate now. Almost every journey of more than ten minutes in duration will involve some kind of traffic jam or hold-up, and there are often no tangible reasons for it. I've been trying to get savvy and find short-cuts, but I inevitably end up in another queue when I try to get back onto my intended route.

The confusing thing for me is how it has got noticeably worse since the end of Ramadan. Before Ramadan was bad enough - during it was absolutely great with everyone going home early - but since the end of it, the number of cars on the road seems to have suddenly doubled, and with all the rain recently it has only made things worse. I don't know if it's because quite a lot of people went away for the summer and are now back, or it could be that thousands more people have arrived to "live the dream". Bugger off! This is my dream, and you're making it crowded!

I'm increasingly thinking about this and other problems. In one respect, I feel quite lucky to live this end of Dubai, where the traffic going to town in the morning and back out on an evening isn't nearly as heavy as the traffic heading in the other direction. But for how long will this last? You only have to look up a bit as you drive around to see all the tower cranes working constantly, and you can't help notice the giant hoardings going up everywhere trumpeting some new mega-development: Sports City, Falcon City of Wonders, The Lagoons, The second Airport, Dubailand....the list goes on and grows seemingly by the day. I don't know what the projections are, but this place could be double the size it is now in a decade's time.

There are promises of new roads and there is a metro system under construction, but I can't help but wonder what it will be like to live and work here in the not-so-distant future. And the nagging question that I can't get over (aside from building all these mega-structures on sand) is: Who is going to live here and what are they going to do?

I'd estimate that roughly sixty percent of those living here now are working in construction: from labourers to the likes of me. What happens when it's finished? A lot of people will have to go home or find something else to do. We are guests, at the end of the day, we are under no illusions. Here to do a job. Of course, there will be service-sector jobs, but what about those being served? Where are they coming from? Who are they? Hey, I'm sure they have a plan here, but I'll be damned if I can see what it is. Yes, there are ports and airports and hotels and theme parks to run, but that won't employ the population of a four-million-plus city, will it?

As far as I'm concerned, I can't see us living here more than the originally-planned two years. I think we will have had enough by then, and may want a bit of a quieter life. I'm enjoying quite a lot about the place, really I am, but now that I've been here a while, the novelty and the sheen have worn off and I'm seeing more and more of the bad things that lie under the surface and don't get advertised. The Honeymoon period is well and truly over.

The whole hypocrisy issue troubles me. Being a liberal/left-winger/commie pinko here isn't a terribly comfortable feeling. I'd bet that even the most rabid capitalist must have their conscience pricked now and again. You end up switching part of yourself off to deal with it when you see the effects (and even benefits) of rampant, naked, unchecked capitalism with very few of the checks and balances that we have in places like the UK. See no evil and so forth. How long I can keep it up for is something that has yet to be determined.

Thursday, December 21, 2006
'Tis the season to be jolly...

Falalalalalala and so on.

Well, what a frankly stupendous and baffling couple of days we've had. It all started on Monday morning when I woke up in AF at 5.30am. I told Teresa and she sighed and said, "Oh God, not again..." or something along those lines. The good thing is, it went back to normal sinus rhythm within three hours after I went back to sleep for a bit. I thought I should see the doctor, so went along to the hospital and he told me that it was probably a mixture of stress (traffic! money! banks! work! visas!) and over-doing the exercise. Well I had gone hard at it in the gym the night before and was shattered. I think that I have been doing too much too soon, so I think I might rein it in a bit.

Anyway, the doc advised me to take the rest of the day off, even though I felt that I should really go to work because work would be getting a bit peeved with all this time off. But I went home in the end and rested up. I had a bout of dodgy old belly that afternoon as well. Dunno if it was IBS or some bug, but it disappeared by the evening.

The evening, now *that* was remarkable. We ended up seeing doctors again, but this time it was Emma who was the patient. Somehow, when our backs were turned for only a few seconds – all it ever takes – she managed to wedge the index finger of her right hand into a kitchen cupboard door hinge and get it stuck. Teresa managed to pull it free and it was cut really badly.

There was a lot of blood, and it didn't look like a plaster would do any good, so we clamped some kitchen towels over her finger and rushed her to the clinic round the corner at the Springs Village complex, where they stitched her up...without anaesthetic.

They needed four people to hold her down while an impatient doctor put the stitches in. Telling a two-year-old to stay still when you're doing what he did is pretty much a waste of effort. Teresa was in the room with her, and I waited outside with Joseph, listening to nearly the heart-rending shrieking and wailing coming from the room. Poor Teresa had to endure her daughter begging her to get them to stop. Both of us would have taken her place if we could have.

After about half an hour of this, I decided to take Joseph and go to the ATM out in the entrance area, across from the Choithrams shop. I needed to get that shrieking out of my head, if only for a moment, and I could sense Joseph was getting upset as well. As we walked out we were hit by a completely unexpected, surreal moment. In the opposite entrance lobby near the shop, there was a grotto of sorts, consisting of random, scary-looking models of animals wearing winter clothes and a scruffy Santa sitting there looking bored beyond tears. There weren't many kids around, and no-one seemed to want to talk to Santa. The sound that reached my ears told me why.

Coming full-blast from a portable stereo was a Christmas song, but it wasn't any Christmas song, it was Kevin Bloody Wilson singing, "Ho, Ho, Fucking Ho, What a Crock of Shit," in his inimitable, Australian style. Santa and his elves stood around completely oblivious to the filth spewing out from the speakers and echoing around the lobby. People ushered their confused young children past as quickly as possible whilst trying to block their ears. After stifling a belly-laugh and remembering I had Joseph with me, I cleared my throat and asked Santa if he knew what the song was about. He was either Lebanese or Syrian, I guess, so didn't understand what the problems was, but then other people started complaining as well and they eventually changed the music. It was so utterly unreal that I wondered afterwards if I had dreamt it all.

When we went back to the clinic the screaming had stopped and it wasn't long before Teresa emerged from the treatment rooms carrying Emma in her arms. Our little daughter was asleep now, completely shattered from her ordeal. Her wounded finger was completely covered in a bundle of white bandages that dwarfed her hand. She slept soundly that night, aided by the wonderful invention that all parents know and love: Calpol.

And then to last night: We had our office Christmas Party at a hotel restaurant where it was seafood buffet night, so the turkey and Brussels sprouts were nowhere to be seen. The wine and beer flowed, the cliques formed onto their own tables, mainly along cultural and ethnic lines followed by seniority. I somehow managed to position myself on the Big Cheese table with a few members of the upper echelons of our company, and even had a brief chat with the MD about my work (good), my health (bad) and my future (who knows?)

When he asked me to give critical feedback I did slip in a mention about the administration problems, but I tried to keep it reasonably polite, constructive and not too strong. He listened and made his own points, but it wasn't long before the conversation moved onto more important issues such as penis-size and the next thing we knew we were participating in a drinking game called The Boat Race, which is basically a line of people downing pints in sequence, and the first line to finish all theirs wins.

From there, it rapidly went downhill. One or two of the staff were starting to get extremely drunk, and one or two were looking to stir up fights. Apart from a few drunken threats and raised voices, nothing really nasty happened, as far as I know, and everyone dispersed into the night, catching taxis home or on to other venues.

For some reason I still can't fathom or excuse, I managed to get press-ganged into moving on to a night-club. I'm just too easily-led for my own good. I wasn't drinking any more alcohol (I'd drunk more than enough, despite telling myself I should only have two glasses of wine) but it was getting late, and I should have called it a night there and then. But no, I gave in and ended up in a club called Rattlesnake.

Rattlesnake sounds dodgy, and it is. Entering the place was like walking into a zombie movie. Under the weird UV lighting every face looked ghostly blue-white with dark, sunken eyes, and as we walked to the bar, desperate hands clawed and pawed at our arms. Instead of, "Brains! Brains!" there was the shrill cry of "Luvyoolongtime. Fiedorra!" or something equally spine-chilling. Thankfully, I saw sense, and extracted myself after one drink, breaking free from the moaning, mewling masses, before clambering into a taxi and speeding home to my waiting bed.

Work today has been a trial and a tribulation. Not really hungover, but really, really tired. Early night for me tonight, methinks.

Monday, December 25, 2006
MERRY CHRISTMAS

Guess what: It's a sunny day. The kids have opened their pressies. We're going for dinner at a hotel in a bit. Merry Christmas, one and all!

Tuesday, December 26, 2006
It's the most wonderful time...

of the day.

Three hours left in this quiet, windowless office. The urge to stuff my face with chocolate is pretty strong. Who works on Boxing Day? What a load of old bollocks. It's a real come-down after the enjoyment of yesterday.

We had a nice time. The kids loved their presents and were full of joy and brightness and all the other things that have slowly been sucked from my soul over the years. Christmas lunch was really quite enjoyable. The venue (Courtyard Marriott at Green Community) was pleasantly decorated and they looked after us terrifically. Our waiter - an Indonesian man named Yoyo (I kid you not) - was a genuinely lovely guy and attentive to our every need, although he was more of an in-and-out than an up-and-down kind of guy.

We were first in, arriving just before 12pm, so had the whole buffet area to ourselves for a bit, until people started filtering in. By 1.30pm the place was full and buzzing with cheerful conversation. We feasted on smoked salmon, turkey, roast ham and Christmas pudding, and it was all really tasty. The only thing missing was stuffing and Brussels sprouts. I miss my sprouts, if not the violent and malodorous effects of them.

Outside, the sun shone high in a warm blue sky. We could see the hotel swimming pool out of the window and there were people sitting out there having a pool-side drink. Some were even having a swim. It felt faintly absurd to be sitting there eating Christmas dinner, pulling crackers and wearing silly paper hats in such a place.

By 3pm, we couldn't force any more food or drink down our gullets, and I was feeling merry enough, so we paid our bill and headed home, weaving through massive queues of lorries and trucks on the Emirates Road. It's just another day for everyone else here.

We spent the evening playing games and ate a late, light tea of a few sandwiches. Phone calls to relatives and friends were made, and it was at that point when Teresa and I realised what we were missing. We chatted via video-link to my parents on Messenger, as they prepared to eat dinner at my uncle and aunt's huge house in Scotland, surrounded by a large contingent of my mother's large family. We spoke to Teresa's parents on the phone, and there was obvious emotion in the voices coming down the lines. These are the times you that miss your family.

So, this morning, I had to get up for work again and face the commute through the blowing sand. It seems a bit pointless, as a lot of people are away, and it is spookily quiet in the office. The locals are gearing up for the next Eid, which happens at the end of the week. We should get a couple of days off round New Year at least.

And there you go. Christmas is done and dusted for another twelve months. I wonder where we will be next year.

Saturday, December 30, 2006

A thought for the New Year.

I found this quote on an internet message board I frequent. I think it's superb, and it resonates with me on a very deep level.

"To be truly challenging, a voyage, like a life, must rest on a firm foundation of financial unrest. Otherwise, you are doomed to a routine traverse, the kind known to yachtsmen who play with their boats at sea... cruising, it is called. Voyaging belongs to seamen, and to the wanderers of the world who cannot, or will not, fit in. If you are contemplating a voyage and you have the means, abandon the venture until your fortunes change. Only then will you know what the sea is all about.

"'I've always wanted to sail to the South Seas, but I can't afford it.' What these men can't afford is not to go. They are enmeshed in the cancerous discipline of security. And in the worship of security we fling our lives beneath the wheels of routine - and before we know it our lives are gone.

"What does a man need - really need? A few pounds of food each day, heat and shelter, six feet to lie down in - and some form of working activity that will yield a sense of accomplishment. That's all - in the material sense, and we know it. But we are brainwashed by our economic system until we end up in a tomb beneath a pyramid of time payments, mortgages, preposterous gadgetry, playthings that divert our attention for the sheer idiocy of the charade.

"The years thunder by, the dreams of youth grow dim where they lie caked in dust on the shelves of patience. Before we know it, the tomb is sealed.

"Where, then, lies the answer? In choice. Which shall it be: bankruptcy of purse or bankruptcy of life?"

Sterling Hayden

JANUARY

Monday, January 01, 2007

HAPPY NEW YEAR...

...from a place without Big Ben and without first footers and all that kind of thing. I can hear some fireworks in the distance; probably at the Burj Al Arab.

Cheers all!

Thursday, January 04, 2007

All is quiet...

...on New Year's Day. A World in Whi-yut gets under way...

New Year in Dubai was different, but then again, what isn't? We treated the kids to a trip to Ski Dubai at the Mall of the Emirates on New Year's Eve, as promised. It was as much a treat for us, actually. The chance to see - albeit artificially rather than naturally-produced - snow and feel cold was too enticing for us after being in a permanent summer since August.

We paid our money, bought gloves and hats, and then went to the clothing counters to be issued with snow boots, socks, trousers and jackets to wear in the snow park. We went along quite early when it wasn't too busy, and before long we were all kitted out like Eskimos. Well, Eskimos with bad taste. I haven't seen many Inuit wearing blue and pink snow-suits. Either way, we ventured through the entry gate to the snow park, then through the first set of sliding doors, which act like an airlock, and finally through another set of sliding doors. A blast of arctic air hit us full in the face, making us shiver. "It's bloody freezing!" was the only thing I could say at this point, stating the bleeding obvious, as always.

And then the fun began. We charged around the snow park with its ice mazes, igloos, sledging hills and toboggan runs. We spotted crowds of people watching us from behind the glass in the main mall, like people watching animals in the zoo. I had to fight back the urge to bare my arse and pee my name in the snow. We climbed up to a small wooden tower and looked up at the incredible sight of people using the ski lift to go up and ski down an enormous four-hundred-metre-long, sixty-metre-high slope that dog-legged halfway up and disappeared into the distance.

I decided to have a go on the toboggan run without wearing gloves and managed to scrape my left hand on the hard ice on the wall of the run. I think I left at least half an inch of skin there. Then I had a shot on the rubber ring run and ended up with two blocks of ice for hands after using them as brakes to prevent myself from sliding into a queue of waiting people. It was around about this point that I remembered that snow is nice in small doses. The best thing about this place was being able to leave the cold behind whenever we wanted.

The kids enjoyed it all though, which was the main aim. After we left and got changed back into "normal" clothes, we headed for lunch at the Alpine-themed St. Moritz café, situated just next to the exit. As we sat there next to a roaring fire (on a TV screen embedded into a fireplace), eating hearty food and drinking steaming mugs of hot chocolate, we looked through the windows back into the snow park, watching men in dish-dashes playing in the snow. The mind boggles when you think about how much energy they must use to keep the place cooled to around freezing point, and even lower when the whole thing closes at night and the snow blowers come on. It sums up what Dubai is about: Surreal excess.

New Year's Eve night was a quiet affair in the main. We let Joseph stay up till midnight, and played Junior Monopoly about half a dozen times. At 11pm a party started in a house to the back of ours, and loud Middle-Eastern-influenced dance music filled the night air with its enchanting, hypnotic rhythms. The time came - midnight passed - and it was eerily quiet for just a moment. I suddenly pined for the sound of Big Ben's chimes to tell us it was here, but there was nothing except a bit of cheering from the party at the back and the sound of distant fireworks at the Burj Al Arab. I bet they looked good.

So we had a mini Auld Lang Syne session, hugged and kissed, put the tired boy to bed and started sending text messages and e-mails to friends and family back in the UK. And then we went to bed. The music from the back didn't really keep us awake; I think it stopped at about 2am.

On New Year's Day we decided to have a big roast chicken dinner with stuffing and Yorkshire puddings and gravy and all that other stuff that we would have at home. But before that we went to Safa Park for a little stroll and some fresh air. I wasn't sure what to expect, and was surprised by the size and scale of the place. There are little gardens, statues, water features and play-parks scattered all over.

There is a central area with a boating lake, a fairground and barbeque areas.

At first I was impressed. The green spaces were large and pleasant and mostly clean. Then we came across the artificial river that runs from the boating lake to a small pond and waterfall and I noticed that the water there was chock-full of plastic carrier bags and other trash. A couple of pissed-off looking ducks sat forlornly in the murky, stagnant water nearby. I wondered how it could have become like that, and why it hadn't been cleaned up, but I soon got something of an answer.

We eventually came to a sand-covered play-park and settled down on a wooden bench while the kids had a play on the swings and roundabouts. As I sat there, my attention was caught by a four or five-year-old child who came up to the edge of the park, holding a packet of mini-Pringles. I watched in disbelief as the child took the crisps in one hand and dropped the packet on the floor with the other before wandering off, as casually as you like. The child's mother, who was sat on the grass behind her, didn't bat an eyelid. Not surprisingly, she was surrounded by half-empty carrier bags, which I wasn't sure she would bother to pick up before she left.

I turned and shook my head and watched another child in the play-park drop an empty drink carton on the sand as he climbed a ladder. I looked round some more and saw pieces of litter everywhere. In the middle of the play-ground there was a bin, so I stood up, picked up the discarded Pringles packet and made a point of placing it in the bin. People around me watched me impassively, unimpressed by my actions.

Cultural differences aside, I find myself wondering about the mentality of some people. They just don't seem to care a jot about things like litter. Doesn't the sight of rubbish all over the place sadden them? Do they think that someone else will just come along and sweep it up?

The rubbish in the pond was the real shocker for me. I'd always thought that we had a bad attitude to litter in the UK, and that other places were invariably cleaner. It might be true of some parts of continental Europe, but it seems that it's actually even worse here. I've been in plenty of parks back home, but I've never seen a sight like I saw in that pond. A bit of litter, yes, but this was really, really bad, and the whole blasé attitude towards the dropping of rubbish on the floor amazed me as well.

Different places have different values and different attitudes, and I understand that this is the case, but sometimes I find myself being surprised by how utterly alien some people's values are to me. How do you reconcile this? Do you just let them get on with it, or do you say something? Is it our right to impose our value system on others, or is it their right to live as they see fit, and how they have lived it all their lives without our interference? When does the line get crossed: when others get hurt or offended? We all know that some people are more easily offended than others, and that different things offend different people, and that right and wrong are not black and white. Oh, it's a moral minefield. I'm rambling and preaching again. I should write a "Sickened of Springs" letter to 7 Days for everyone to laugh and point at.

After the fun of play-park we went on a boat ride on the lake where there was no littler, and hired a little replica ferry for the four of us. I took charge naturally. I didn't think it was going to take my bulk when I boarded as it pitched and wobbled perilously, but we managed to stay afloat and spent a dizzying twenty minutes going round in circles, chasing seagulls and avoiding the locals who sped round in circular hovercraft-style vessels. They drive boats like they drive cars, is all I will say.

On the way out of the park, I remembered hearing someone talking on the radio about the pleasures of walking barefoot on grass, so I took my shoes and socks off, before strolling across the cool, lush grass. It was marvellous. I was just glad that they don't allow dogs in the park. Joseph challenged me to a race, and I found myself sprinting across the grass after him, and actually catching him. This was a new experience for me, because I haven't been able to run that fast for a long, long time. I haven't been able to keep up with Joseph for a while, but on New Year's Day, I was running, maybe not like the wind, more like a stiff breeze, and it felt good. The weight loss and exercise *has* made a difference. It's a shame my Perthes-disease-damaged hip won't tolerate much real running, because I could get myself fit in no time at all. Ah well, maybe when I get my bionic leg, eh?

Oh, yeah, and the roast chicken dinner was fabulous.

Thursday, January 11, 2007

You know how it was quiet?

Well, since then I've had a bit of a week, I can tell you.

My health problems continue to annoy and frustrate me (along with the frustration of dealing with banks in this country) and I have been in hospital again for various tests and something-oscopies galore.

I am beginning to think that these things all linked, actually. I'm not the most easy-going of folk, as I might sometimes allude to with my rambling rants, and I tend to let things wind me up a tad. The last month has seen some really frustrating episodes, with trying to get car loans and finalising visas and various other things. So, it's probably no coincidence that my gastric reflux has been playing hell with me and that in turn plays hell with my arrhythmia, triggering ectopic beats and short runs of AF. The cycle of worry spirals downwards in ever-decreasing circles.

I finally managed to convince my cardiologist that I needed referring to another doctor about the reflux, and the new doctor was only too keen to stick cameras into every orifice available. Fortunately the insurance company only authorised the endoscopy, which is the one down the top end.

I've had a colonoscopy before, and believe me when I say that it ain't pleasant. Not only did I have to starve myself for a day, I also had to take industrial-strength laxatives that rapidly compelled me to sit on the porcelain throne for hours with a roll of chilled toilet roll. Then at the hospital, I had to have an enema using cold water, before losing what was left of my dignity as I lay on my side in an ill-fitting hospital gown and having a long black tube forced up my arse. The only blessing was the sedative, which wasn't that strong last time, because I felt a considerable amount of discomfort. Even so, in my sedated state, I was half-expecting Lloyd Grossman to appear on the monitor screen and say, "Hooow liyuvs in an arse like thus..?"

As it was, I only had to do the endoscopy this time, and they must have used some good shit on me, because I was out like a light only a minute or so after they injected the sedative. I have a fuzzy, vague memory of the nurse putting some kind of guard in my mouth and strapping it round my head, then there was a little bit of gagging as they put the endoscope in, but then nothing. When the doctor said, "Bring out the Gimp", I think I may well have been dreaming.

I woke up after an hour of dreamless, blissful sleep to see Teresa, Joseph and Emma sat next to me, and I wondered what they had been saying about me. I had a chicken sandwich and a few more minutes sleep, then after a quick chat with the doctor they gave me a DVD showing what they had done and let me go. I had an ever-so-slightly sore throat, but nothing untoward, and before long we were on our way home.

At home I watched the DVD, and was treated to the sight of my insides being explored. It was quiet interesting, and not too scary until this little metal pincer device appeared at the bottom of the picture to take biopsies of my acid-scarred digestive tract. I say little, but on a large TV it looked massive, and reminded my of Ridley Scott's Alien taking chunks out of people's heads and chests with its extendable mandibles. When the pincers withdrew there was blood, and the sight of this made me shudder somewhat. I'm glad that I was asleep when it actually happened.

The diagnosis is that I have something called Barrett's oesophagus, which has absolutely nothing to do with cheap shoes or identikit houses. The doctor casually told me that it is a pre-cancerous condition where the lining of the oesophagus has been eroded and is changing in cellular structure. It has to be managed and monitored very carefully, which involved more drugs, more endoscopies at regular intervals, and avoidance of certain types of food; naturally the nice ones like chocolate, coffee and red wine. So if I want to live a long, healthy life I have to live it like a monk; a monk that doesn't attend communion, that is. Losing more weight will help matters too. Oh well, I did want to lose weight, and I still am, despite having a slight break from the diet over Christmas.

Drugs, drugs, drugs. The oesophagus doc gave me two more types to take, and I happily added them to the list. I have had to create a plethora of reminders on my mobile phone's calendar, which now bleeps at me at certain points in the day to remind me to take the tablets for my blood pressure, my arrhythmia, my cholesterol, my nightly happy pill and now for my bad belly.

All was well until Sunday when I noticed that I felt rotten, and really tired; more so than is usual for me. I thought it was probably the after-effects of the sedative, so took the day off. But on Monday I felt even worse, and was starting to wonder what was going on. I was actually physically shaking by this point, and aching all over. I wanted to sleep all the time, but when I lay down, I just couldn't get comfortable.

So I went back to the hospital to see my doctors. They did the usual tests: blood pressure, bloods, ECG and so on. They found nothing. Then, in a stroke of luck, I happened to bump into the doctor who had done the endoscopy, and when I showed him the contents of the bag of all the drugs I had brought with me, he took a disconcerting, sharp intake of breath and told me to stop taking one of the drugs straight away. Then I saw the heart doctor and he halved the dosage of a couple of the other meds.

It worked. Now I just feel crappy again, rather than utterly rotten. The whole episode has been a little disturbing if I'm honest. I have said before that I have been impressed with the medical facilities here so far, and you can't fault the level of attention that you get. You can see a doctor any time of night or day, and at weekends, and you don't have to wait weeks and months for an appointment with a specialist.

The down-side is that you are seen maybe *too* quickly, and with profit margins being a major factor in the private sector, however much you try and dress it up, the bottom line is what ultimately matters. There is always the potential for these kind of medication mistakes (not to mention others) to be made.

The liaison between the different doctors seemed to be limited to an initial referral, and then it was up to me to keep each doctor informed of what the other was up to. That isn't my job. In the UK a General Practitioner would normally take an overview, and every time you see a new specialist you have to tell them your whole medical history and tell them what drugs you're on (which takes me a while, unsurprisingly). A friend in Dubai has said that this is par for the course in these parts, and advised me to get second opinions on any major diagnoses that I get. I'm starting to wonder if he might be right. I'm just thankful that my level of awareness (some might call it paranoia) on these matters brought about a swift end to the problem.

By Tuesday I was feeling right again. And then the unthinkable started to happen. The stresses and frustrations looked like they were leaving town. The fates have started shifting, and I might just get my finances sorted and get the car loan I've been trying to get for a month now. Thanks to certain people at my company I should now be able to sort out the payment cycle problems and remedy the knock-on effects of the late salary payment in November and December. I can start to enjoy living here instead of banging my head against the wall and worrying about bouncing a cheque and ending up in clink. You read right: bouncing cheques is a criminal offence here.

It's a bloody good job that things are finally moving, because in little more than three weeks we have our first visitors coming from the UK. Teresa's mother and sister are coming to stay with us for three weeks in February. I want everything to be in place for their arrival, and fingers crossed, it's starting to look like it will.

Of course, there will be more glitches and hitches and hiccups. When I got home last night after a good day, Emma was in the process of vomiting copiously. It seems she has a touch of gastroenteritis, bless her. Teresa slept in her room with her last night after taking her to the doctors and getting a pile of medication for her. I checked it thoroughly for anything dodgy-looking. She's never been sick like this in her short life, never had anything worse than a cough and cold, so I imagine it's as confusing and scary for her as it is worrying for us.

In the UK it was Joseph who was always getting sickness bugs. Almost every month he would start throwing up, usually in the car on the way to Middlesbrough, strangely. What with her cut finger and now this, she's had a hard time since arriving in Dubai. Fingers crossed it'll get better for her.

Friday, January 19, 2007
Money, money, money

I have finally had my car loan approved. I've been trying for about a month to get one, ever since I got my residence visa, and yesterday the money was credited to my account. Now I can get the two cars I need. The relief! It's nearly as good as coming out of Atrial Fibrillation.

I have made myself ill over it all, and in hindsight I shouldn't have, but when you come up against the incompetence, intransigence and sheer bloody-minded bureaucracy that I've encountered over the last month or two, I defy anyone to remain calm.

Today, as something of a celebration, we went for brunch at Mina A'Salam, a hotel at the Madinat Jumeirah. It has had a lot of good write-ups, and it was fantastic. I'm still stuffed five hours after eating. The kids were well catered for as well, and even though it was quite pricey, the free-flowing booze and really high-quality food made it all worthwhile.

The ambience there is really special, and the Madinat is probably one of my favourite places in Dubai. I can't wait to take some of our guests there when they come to visit. My doctors probably won't be happy that I've had a few glasses of wine, but I've not had any for at least three weeks, and probably won't have any more for a good while now....a little of what you fancy, and all that.

The whole bank episode is in the past now. Let's move on. Another week has zipped by in the blink of an eye. We are busy at work again, and it shows. The spirits of people in the office are dipping badly again, so much so that the newest of the staff have noticed it.

It doesn't help that the office manager has been on the rampage this week. Before Christmas he delivered a *fatwa* on people not wearing ties, and this week he has been cracking down on early lunch leavers and anyone with the notion of having a life outside of work.

A couple of his comments this week have left me bamboozled. He suggested (half-jokingly, I hope) that the lives of my family were unimportant when there were important clients to be placated, and then when someone had to cancel some leave, he said he didn't have *any* sympathy, because holidays were more of a privilege than a right, especially as *he* has worked years with only two days of leave.

That's all fair and well, and may impress someone somewhere, but for the rest of us, work is a means to an end. I work to live, not vice-versa. I will give my all and put my best in at the office, and have no qualms about doing a bit of work outside my allotted hours and travelling to places like Doha for a few days should the need arise, but when the implication is that work comes first, second and third, with family life a poor fourth, I start to get worried.

There are people in this world who like to come to work at 7am and leave at 8pm, and they make it out to be some kind of macho honour thing, but to me that's nothing more than bullshit. You can only be effective for so long during a day, and nine hours is about right. I will take a lunch break, and I will leave work at 6pm, unless, as I say, there is an urgent job that *needs* to be done. If we feel obliged to stay long hours or are made to feel guilty for not doing so, I honestly think it makes for bad morale. But there we are, and there we go. It pays the bills, and the work is quite interesting, and I'm sure it could be worse. I've learned loads since I came here, and the CV will not suffer with the scale and type of project I'm working on now.

I'm going to shoot off an a slight tangent now, but one thing I've started to notice at work and even in general is the behaviour of some people here, in particular Western expats. I've noticed the way some of these people talk to and behave towards people of other nationalities here, especially those from the Indian sub-continent or the Philippines. Not to beat about the Dubya: they treat them like dirt. They shout at and berate them for the slightest lapse in standards of service, they show no gratitude or even basic manners towards them, and seem to think they are perfectly entitled to lord it over these people. They wouldn't get away with it at home, because they'd get told where to go forth and procreate, I have not a shred of doubt.

The thing is, it's a double-edged sword, because the people on the receiving end just take it, giving it the, "Yes, sir/madam," in their whiny American accent before scurrying away sheepishly when they've been reprimanded by another highly-strung, self-important expat. Some of them look petrified when you talk to them, and then they look genuinely astonished when you say "Please" and "Thank You" to them, before breaking into a broad smile.

I often wonder how much these people resent us moneyed westerners, especially when we act like complete and utter twats towards them. I really want to be there when one of them finally cracks, and tells some jumped-up, beetroot-faced, flip-flop-wearing fool that they added their own special ingredient to the drink they've just guzzled greedily.

Yes, I have witnessed poor service in the past here (especially with the bank!), and yes, I've admitted that I get annoyed and wound up, but when I talk to people I'm doing business with I always try to remain calm and composed and respectful without raising my voice. I usually rant and rave about it to myself afterwards, because rude, arrogant behaviour towards some poor sod when it's probably not even his fault just breeds resentment and contempt and is unlikely to achieve any improvement in service.

It seems to be a pattern here. People change when they come here, and do stuff they wouldn't dream of doing back home, like employing a maid who gets paid a pittance and lives in a single, small room at the back of the villa somewhere. Of course, it's a different country, and a different lifestyle, and as the old saying (or poor excuse) goes: When in Rome. But people here don't do what Romans do, they behave like spoiled brats. I've witnessed expats who don't secure their young children in car seats before driving on the third deadliest roads in the world. I've seen people who seem to think it's perfectly fine to drink drive on a regular basis, and when I say drink - I mean *drink*. I know of at least one instance of someone leaving the scene of an accident because they were drunk when they had a bump.

This happens despite the fact that the punishments here are more severe than back home. It's as if coming to this place makes these people take leave of their senses. Is the almost-permanent sunshine melting their brain cells? Hard to say, really, but as with most things, it's probably a combination of things. As long as they can get away with it, they'll do it. And no amount of tutting, sighing and halo-polishing will change that. I'm no angel, but I would like to think I was brought up right. Or maybe I'm just soft as shite.

I think the funniest thing about it all is when I hear some expat say to me that they came here to get away from all the immigrants who don't respect or integrate with the British Way Of Life, and they particularly hate the mythical PC brigade that pander to their every whim. So they come to a county which is eighty percent immigrant and does quite a lot to accommodate Westerners and their worldly ways. They can come here and lord it over the non-white immigrants, and it makes them feel big and clever, like old-fashioned colonial masters.

Of course, unless they are particularly stupid, they should know the score in terms of their place in society. Westerners are strictly second tier citizens here, sitting in Business Class on Dubai Airways. Locals are in First Class, and there are no upgrades to First Class, under any circumstances. It's only a fool who forgets this. Most of the time things work just fine. The people at the back, in cattle class hate those in front of them; the people in First hate those behind them; and the people in Business hate everyone, but they all tolerate the status-quo because they all know they need each other. Of course, if the Economy class passengers got off the plane, the plane would nose-dive and the whole system would collapse, but they won't because they know there are millions waiting in the wings to take their place for a slice of the action.

Still, with all this said, I still feel happier than I have for a long, long time. Now that I have my visa and the bank worries are behind me, life here is pretty good in the main. Business Class isn't too bad at all...as long as they keep the curtains shut so we can't see what's behind us. Nothing will ever be perfect, but you have to make the best of it, and I think that's what we are doing. I've spent too much time in my life sweating the small stuff.

Sunday, January 28, 2007

Knowing the Drill

It's been a while - again. Time seems to be squeezing together like some mad accordion played by Buster Bloodvessel, and everyday occurrences are just flowing down the drain. We are nearly in February 2007. Yesterday it was June 1996, I'm sure it was. I've already been in Dubai for six months, and it's been a veritable BLEEEUURRRGH.

Still, it's good to be occupied rather than bored. Boredom depresses me and makes me want to eat bad, bad things that will make me fatter again. With all the time in the gym and with Teresa becoming a cyber-addict (she's been playing a particularly annoying and addictive game called Zookeeper pretty much every waking hour...she didn't notice what I did to her the other week while she was sat playing...maybe she'll notice when the bump gets between her and the table in about four or five months' time...) I've had less time to go on the computer. But that's probably a good thing. I spend all day on the bloody things at work.

I'm still going to the good old gymnasium. I've been going for a two full weeks now after joining up at the local place in Springs Village, and the weight is dropping off. I've settled on a nice, short programme that gets me working hard but minimises actual gym time. The best bit about this gym is that it is quiet. I rarely, if ever, have to wait to go on a machine. I am 15kg (33lbs) down now, 23kg (51lbs) to go to reach my target. I like the metric system: the numbers sound much less. At one kilo a week, I should be down to target by July or August. I went to see the heart doctor again last week and he seems to be happy with what I'm doing. Getting drug-free six months down the line would be brilliant.

In other news, we finally got the two cars we've been waiting for so long to get our hands on. The actual buying process was smooth and trouble-free. Once the car dealer had the money, they arranged the insurance and registration for us, and I picked them up the next day. At the same time, Teresa and the kids' residence visas came through, so we got Teresa her driving licence and got rid of the two hire cars. Now, in a weird kind of juxtaposition, I (the large man) drive a little sporty coupe car and she (the little lady) drives a seven-seater MPV. We bought second-hand, of course. Buying new is a waste of time...you're just as well to take twenty thousand quid out of the bank and set fire to five of it, in my humble opinion.

I'm now driving more like a local. I flash my lights and beep my horn and occasionally weave between lanes when I get frustrated at the chap in the ageing white Nissan Sunny bumbling along at 80kph in the middle lane without a care in the world. But I'm getting to thinking that it's the only way to be, because hesitancy here can get you into bother.

Of course, I draw the line at some things. I always strap the children into their seats nice and safely. I never drive on the hard shoulder. I don't send SMS messages whilst driving at 180kmph, and I'll never, *ever* plaster pictures of my country's leaders on my car's back window. Can you imagine seeing that in the UK? I reckon anyone who put Tony Blair's insincere grin on the back window would probably get a brick through it.

As I drive around this place and get used to the anarchy on the highways, I'm starting to realise that a lot of the people in this part of the world live in little sealed-off bubbles. It's not malicious, they just don't think about consequences, particularly when other people are involved. The oft-used phrase, "*Insha'allah*" is starting to make a little bit of sense. It's the culture, the upbringing to just carry on regardless, and leave the worrying about it all to God. Yes, it is a way of passing on responsibility, but then it also means less worry and stress. I could learn something there, for sure.

It was similar in Taiwan. The people were lovely and friendly and hospitable, as they are here most of the time, but when they get in a car or into some public space where they are just an anonymous face, they throw a switch and the bubble surrounds them. They must wonder what these flashing orange light things and shiny, reflective appendages attached to the doors are, because they don't bloody use them. And they have no idea what queuing is.

And then there was the Incident with the Drill, which completely threw me out of kilter the other night. I think it was Thursday. I was sat at my laptop at home, minding my own business. It was late. Teresa had gone to bed. From nowhere, the incredibly loud and wall-juddering sound of an electric drill on hammer setting burst into life. I looked at my watch: it was 11.25pm. Someone next door (in the adjoining villa that's been empty for three months) was obviously moving in, and had decided that this was the right time to start auditioning for DIY SOS. I can't remember the exact thoughts that were going through my mind, but I think the words "what", "the" and "fuck," were in there somewhere, amongst others.

I let it go. I ignored it. It couldn't go on all night. Could it? Teresa, Joseph and Emma didn't seem to be overly upset by it upstairs. The kids could sleep on the runway at DXB International Airport (or Mirdiff, as it is known round here). It kept going for another half an hour, on and off, and finally ceased just before midnight. It's a good job they stopped, because I was getting more and more annoyed, and was even thinking about going to bed in a bad mood.

Again, I put this behaviour down those cultural quirks I was talking about before: that unwitting, benign selfishness. It was like my first few weeks in Dubai, which I spent in that flea-pit of a hotel, trying to get some sleep with all the banging doors and shouting and general hoo-hah that occurred every night after midnight. It's not malicious. These people have just been brought up that way, and don't know any different.

The next day, as we pulled out of our car port and set off for Al Ain, we saw the culprit getting out of his own car with some curtain poles.

It was a Westerner.

Looking for planes in Al Ain.

Does it rain much in Al Ain? Well, Al Ain very green; there are trees and grass everywhere. But then it could be down to the irrigation. I don't really know how these oasis locations work, if I'm honest. I should've paid more attention in geography lessons at school.

After leaving the nocturnal driller to his curtain poles, we headed out of town. It was high time to get out of the place again, and we had juggled the idea of Fujairah on the East coast, or Al Ain, which is down on the Oman border in the Emirate of Abu Dhabi. Both were a fair drive away, but the lines on our map showed an easier route to Al Ain, so we headed there. There was an Air Show on at Al Ain as well.

I wish we'd gone to Fujairah now.

The drive was pleasant enough, if a little boring. The long, straight roads are easy enough to drive on, even if they provide little in the way of stimulus for the kids. We noticed that the signs and petrol station names changed as we entered the next Emirate. All of them were the same name, in fact, and every single one was an exact replica of the one before. I started to wonder if we were going round in circles.

Before long, the harsh, red sand of the desert became increasingly punctuated by lush, green vegetation. We aren't talking about planted palm trees and imported grass, either. Verdant pastures passed by in a green blur, and trees of all kinds cropped up in little clumps. It's quite a thing to see after being in the dusty, landscaped confines of Dubai for so long.

We arrived at Al Ain's outskirts and were greeted by the sight of a giant Arabic coffee pot in the middle of a roundabout, similar to the ones they have in Doha. We started following the signs for the Airport, which I figured is the kind of place they usually host Air shows.

After several miles of outer suburbs and no sign of an airport, never mind an aeroplane, we decided to head into the town centre and get something to eat. We passed more trees and greenery as we drove through pleasant suburbs, and noticed that there wasn't one skyscraper on the horizon, with no building higher than three or four storeys. There was not one tower crane to be seen, either. Evidently Al Ain is complete.

After finding that the town's eponymous Mall was basically shut (and once again getting lost in the car park thanks to misleading signs), we found another Mall in an area called Al Jimi, which was open, and had lunch in the food court. With our light lunch in our stomachs, we had a wander and a window shop. Marvellous: We came all the way to Al Ain for a change of scenery, and ended up in a bloody shopping Mall.

I decided to put an end to this abject silliness and we headed out again to see if we could find the airport. We did, and were greeted by the sight of thousands of cars parked in every conceivable location alongside the roads approaching the airport, and about three aging aeroplanes parked on the airport apron. A short drive around the airport roads took us into a long queue for the main parking area, which was full. This is what happens when you turn up halfway through the day.

As we waited for the queue to move, we watched a yellow bi-plane performing a startling array of aerial stunts, swooping, rolling and diving towards earth. As I wondered if the pilot was sending SMS messages whilst flying, I suddenly remembered why I didn't have much time for Air Shows, specifically aerobatic displays by daredevil pilots flying very fast jet planes directly towards each other. I had lived in Germany near a US airbase in the late 1980s, and at the peak of the annual Air Show there had been an awful mid-air collision during such an aerobatics display that had sent a plane into the crowd, killing around fifty people. If we hadn't been away on holiday at the time, we may well have been there when it happened, and ever since then, I just haven't felt comfortable watching planes doing tricks. It's bad enough when they fly in a nice straight line, thank you very much, and really bad when they fly towards each other at high speed. I hate to say it, but even the Red Arrows fill me with dread.

As it was, the whole spectacle looked decidedly underwhelming, and with it getting on in the day, and with parking options looking limited, we decided to head back to Dubai. On the way back, as we left Al Ain's green plains behind, I spotted a sign for the East Coast, and realised it would have been the better option. Yes, Al Ain is different to Dubai, but ultimately it was a bit bland, and didn't seem to offer much to the family. You live and learn, I suppose.

The kids were good, though. They spent a long time in the car without causing too much of a scene, so we went to a Wild West-themed family-friendly (i.e. full of *other* people's screaming brats) restaurant for tea when we got back as a treat (and I fancied some pork ribs as well). They enjoyed it, even if the ribs weren't much to write home about...Dear Mum, having a splendid time. The ribs aren't very good, though.

Now we are focused on next weekend, and the imminent arrival of Teresa's mum and older sister. Teresa and kids are really excited, and so am I. It will be good to see some familiar faces after so long.

Monday, January 29, 2007
Only in Dubai

Today I saw and heard of three things that made me shake my head and say, "Only in Dubai", which seems to be quite a popular phrase these days.

1. I saw a lovely new, shiny silver BMW 7 series covered in red, white, green and black heart-shaped stickers.

2. I heard on the radio that an ambulance attending an emergency took eighteen minutes to travel half a kilometre on the approach to the Arabian Ranches roundabout. No-one would move to let it past.

3. I saw a man dressed up as Charlie Chaplin walking next to an Arab man in Ibn Battuta Mall.

Wednesday, January 31, 2007
The Bloke in the Bubble

The UAE national football team has won the Gulf Cup, beating Oman 1-0 in last night's final in Abu Dhabi. Good stuff. Now I understand why that BMW I saw the other day was covered in red, white, green and black heart stickers. No window flags for this lot - they go the whole hog, even if it causes permanent damage to their expensive motors.

Today I saw even more bizarre decorations on cars, with spray paint in the national colours applied graffiti-style to wheels, body and even windows. Streamers hung on every available appendage - door handles, aerials, window wipers - I get the impression they're quite happy about it all. There are reports of cars careering up and down various roads with people perched on top waving flags and blowing horns until the wee hours. I can't imagine there were many drunken brawls, to be fair.

Speaking of cars, I've been observing more of the Bubble behaviour that I was talking about recently, where the people here just seem to seal themselves away from all external influence and show no consideration for anyone or anything. Like I've said, I don't think there's an ounce of malice in it at all; it's just the way it is. And to be honest, it isn't just the locals. Expats start to assimilate this behaviour after a while.

Imagine the average day of a person living here, whether they be Arab or Indian or whatever. He or she drives to work at 180kmph (or 60kmph in the fast lane in a Nissan Sunny in the case of older Indians), merrily sending SMS messages and flipping the headlight stick on the steering column as they go. When they get close to their turn off, they cut across three or four lanes at the last possible minute, as if they weren't expecting it, causing a cacophony of angry horns and desperately squealing brakes from the cars around them.

He or she arrives at work, and proceeds to park their car diagonally across two or even three spaces. Then they get out of the car and saunter into the office building, eyes still fixed on their mobile phone. They press the lift call button a dozen times and wait impatiently, now talking to someone on their hands-free kit as they tap their foot on the floor. Then the lift arrives with a merry ping, the doors open, and they barge straight into the lift without waiting for anyone who might want to exit to come out. As the lift rises, they have a good, long, loving look at themselves in the mirror.

The lift arrives at their floor, and he or she rushes headlong out into the corridor before deciding to visit the facilities / rest-rooms / bogs (delete as appropriate). If you're behind them, you'd better watch out. Don't assume that they will hold the door for the person directly behind. Some will, but most will just let it slam into your face. Then (if you're a bloke) you watch them approach the row of three urinals on the wall…

This bit really gets me. I just find it sums everything up. In the UK, we have this little game with urinals, where the first person to approach always takes one at either end; never in the middle. No-one, but no-one, wants to stand directly next to another man having a slash.

But not here.

Here, the first man to the urinal invariably takes the middle station and stands there with feet planted as wide apart as possible, doing his business without a care in the world. If I come in behind him, I don't know what to do. I just can't bring myself to stand right next to them, even if there's room because of that afore-mentioned wide stance, so I end up going into the cubicles and feeling faintly ridiculous for doing so. What am I afraid of...seeing or being seen? It's a British thing.

Then, when you come out, the person is at the sink, and they are either snorting water up their nose, hacking up massive lumps of phlegm with that charming "*hkhkhkhkhkhkooooocccckkkk*" noise, or they are performing a contortionist act to wash their feet in the sink. From there, they go to their office and spend the rest of the day smoking in the no-smoking areas of the building and drinking one cup of coffee after another.

Of course, it's all an education, and demonstrates something - possibly that us Brits are really anal and uptight. Cultures are all different and this place is the biggest melting pot of all, and somehow we muddle through. We shake our heads and swap anecdotes about what the locals and sub-cons and Filipinos do and laugh about it with our mates, but ultimately we just get on with it. I suppose because we have to. I imagine the other ethnicities laugh at our little foibles as well.

I hope this doesn't come across as critical of the people I'm watching. It isn't. It's just the observations of a man who has been brought up in that stiff, British way, and I find these little behavioural quirks alien and fascinating. I really dread finding myself saying those tell-tale words: "I'm not racist, but..."

I think that deep down we are all basically the same. We all breathe and eat and sleep and love and hate. We are all born and we all die. When you cut us, we bleed. But differences are there for a reason. We all live in different places with different influences, and they affect us all in different ways. And anyway, if we were all exactly the same, life would be boring, and I wouldn't have anything to write about in here.

FEBRUARY

Thursday, February 08, 2007

The Road to Heck

This morning, on my drive to work, I am feeling quite pensive. It may well have been all that wine I drank at last night's BBQ.

My drive of around thirty minutes takes me along the Al Khail road, Sheik Zayed Road's calmer, parallel sibling, and I drive past ever-shrinking patches of desert that probably won't be around for much longer. I drive past stark, skeletal electricity pylons that follow the road, watching the pencil-line cables rise and fall between the pylons as I go. I see tower cranes emerging from the midst of the myriad new developments in the distance, and every few kilometres there seems to be another concrete batching plant surrounded by fleets of dusty concrete mixer trucks.

As I leave behind the huddle of sandy warehouse buildings that make up the Al Quoz Industrial area, the half-built towers of Business Bay and the enormous Burj Dubai development shimmer into view on my left. On the right I pass the Nad Al Sheba racetrack, and if I'm lucky, I may spot small groups of camels galloping along in their awkward but fluid style, training with their R2-D2-style robot jockeys atop their backs.

Soon I turn off the Al Khail Road and head towards the Oud Metha side of the creek. This road then sweeps up and over the road I've just left in a gentle arc and past the Ras Al Khor widlife sanctuary to my right. This is where the creek ends in a shallow, wide lagoon where thousands of pink, statuesque flamingos stand in the water amongst low, thick copses of trees, completely oblivious to the traffic that rumbles by.

A little farther on I pass the newly-opened man-made extension of the Creek, and spot the towers at the Trade Centre end of Sheik Zayed Road sprouting from a dirty brown blanket of smog, and finally the huge, golden pyramid of the nearly-complete Raffles hotel appears, heralding the last few kilometres of my journey, and after another five or so minutes, I'm sat in my windowless office, starting up my computer and waiting for the e-mails to flood in.

Dubai; the shiny new city in the sand. There's nowhere quite like it.

Sunday, February 11, 2007
Making a Splash.

The in-laws are finally here. They've been here a week already, actually, and I think they're enjoying the experience. Caroline, my mother-in-law, has had her first ever experiences of flying and her first ever trip outside the UK, so I imagine it's all very strange and exciting for her. Teresa's sister, Anne, visited the US when I was working there, so she knows about flying, but is obviously excited to be in Dubai, as well as being happy to see us all again, I hope.

Of course, things are even more exciting when you end up doing the unexpected. It all started on Friday. I decided to take them to the Marriott hotel over in Deira for their marvellously mad twelve-hour brunch. I'm regretting it now, because my self-control went right out of the window (or should I say overboard?), and I ate far too much. Teresa and I even tried oysters for the first time, and they weren't as bad as I thought they might be: a bit like salty snot, really. I'm not really selling them well here, am I?

The best feature of this brunch is the ability to leave the hotel for a break from the gluttony and go back for more. They give you a nightclub-style wristband to show the staff, and mark you out as a greedy git. We ate till about 2.30pm, when we were merrily stuffed, then got back in the car and headed to the creek. I thought a little ride on an *abra* would a good experience for both the visitors and for us before we headed back for a second shot at the brunch buffet. You have to get your money's worth, right?

We parked in a scruffy multi-storey car park on the Deira side and walked to the Old Souk *Abra* Station. As soon as we got close, a little Indian man was in amongst our group, beckoning us to his vessel. I said we just wanted to cross the creek, in the way everyone else does. It's a form of public transport, and costs less than 1 dirham for the short trip across the creek, but after a little bit of conferring and haggling, we decided to accept his offer of a short private cruise up and down the creek. It was only going to cost about ten pounds sterling.

It was a good decision. We were soon aboard the small, low vessel, sitting on the raised middle deck area, shaded from the sun by the tarpaulin canopy over our heads. The man relaxed back into his chair, which was set into a hole in the centre of the deck, controlling the wheel with his foot as we sauntered lazily along the creek, taking in the changing views on each side; the Deira side with its glass-fronted towers and Architect's wet dreams, getting taller and more modern as we headed inland; the Bur Dubai side a hotchpotch of sandy-coloured mosques, souks and warehouses.

On either side of the creek itself, we saw the dark, curved forms of traditional dhows packed together tightly at the quaysides and wharfs, unloading their goods, flags flapping in the breeze. The sun shone, the water sparkled, a gentle wind played across our faces, and hundreds of gulls swooped and dodged around us as we chugged along. I turned to Caroline and remarked that while this was very pleasant, I wouldn't want to go in the water here. It didn't look very clean. Prophetic words or what?

Eventually we turned back and headed to the Abra station on the Bur Dubai side. We disembarked, thanked our *abra* man, and headed straight into the hustle and bustle of a real souk. Crowds of passive, staring men swarmed through the darkened, covered alleys. Other men stood next to their stalls and shops, calling out in various languages depending on who they spotted passing by. The few westerners here were greeted with the enthusiastic cries of, "Special price! Very nice! You like?"

We passed through the souk, and then turned back to look at a bejewelled, orange shoulder bag that Teresa had spotted at an earlier stall. I couldn't resist the chance to have a good haggle, so took charge of affairs, and after assuring the vendor that I was not just a tourist, I managed to secure nearly twenty percent off the original price for the bag.

With our purchase secured we decided to head back towards the *abra* station and back over the creek. This time we didn't take a private charter, and sat on another little boat with about thirty other people. As we set off, the *abra* drivers hooted horns at each other to avoid any undue collisions.

And all was good, until we reached the other side.

As we disembarked amongst the throng, the little *abra* bobbed about in the choppy waters and moved back and forth towards from the low, wooden jetty. Caroline helped Joseph onto the jetty, and just as she went to step across, the boat moved away from the jetty, and she lost her footing. I won't forget the look of horror on her face as she plunged into the creek between the boat and the jetty, and I won't forget the panicked scream coming from Teresa's mouth as she watched her mother (who can't swim) creating a splash.

Luckily the gap wasn't very wide, and Caroline had the foresight to stick her arms out as she fell and hold onto each side. I was joined by several other men in swooping to her aid and we soon plucked her out of the creek. I actually had hold of Emma before this happened, and let her hand go momentarily as I bent to help Caroline. In the back of my mind, I hoped someone else had taken Emma's hand. I imagined myself having to jump in the creek to rescue more people. Luckily, Anne was right behind me and had grabbed her.

Caroline was fine. Teresa threw protective arms around her, and looked pretty scared by what had happened. Caroline turned round towards me and started laughing. She was soaked from the waist down, and had a few scrapes under her arms, but she was otherwise fine. We checked the shoulder bag she was carrying (waterproof, luckily) to make sure the passports were still there, and it wasn't until later that we realised she had lost her glasses when she fell in.

Caroline needed a change of clothes, and we were quite a way from home. Caroline didn't want to go home and spoil everyone's fun, so insisted that we went shopping. After a fruitless wander around the shops near the creek, we ended up driving to a Marks and Spencers near the Marriott, where we managed to find some. Good job there was a sale on. By the time this was all sorted we were ready to head back to the buffet, and a few stiff drinks were had.

To her credit, Caroline found the whole episode quite amusing, and by the end of the evening we were all making jokes about swimming and splashing and fish wearing glasses. Teresa and Joseph were the ones who seemed most upset about it. Joseph thought it was his fault somehow, because he was being helped off the boat when it happened. I think the idea of the fish with the glasses on cheered him up.

That night, after driving home from the Marriott, we were all worn out, and everyone had an early night.

Yesterday, we headed for the Madinat Jumeirah. I realise now, after exploring the real souks near the Creek, that the Madinat is just the safe, sterile, Disney-fied version of Dubai. It dresses itself up as an authentic Arabian experience, with the souk-style covered alleyways, sand-coloured wind towers, and even the little waterways and *abras* transporting people around the complex. You soon come to realise that it's all just a big fake. For starters, the souk is air-conditioned and the crowds are much smaller. The people in the crowds are different as well; it's full of well-fed, well-dressed locals and white-faced westerners and with money to burn.

Antique shops and fashion boutiques selling expensive wares line the alleys, alongside charming stalls selling genuine trinkets made in China and other up-market tat. Starbucks and Costa coffee joints invite you in at every turn, and on the lower promenade levels, flashy, well-presented restaurants selling foods from all over the world beckon the tourists wishing to sit out in the fine weather and experience the lifestyle. It's all very safe, all very clean and all very surreal, like looking at the real deal through magic spectacles. I would implore anyone coming to Dubai to see both sides of the souk experience. It tells you everything you need to know.

Tuesday, February 20, 2007
On Safari

The weeks continue to hurry by, with work and play keeping us busy. Early last week, I met up with a friend from my days in Taiwan who was in town on business, and ended up drinking a fair amount of gin and shooting the shit all evening; just like the good old days. Later in the week I was called into the boss's office, and despite my initial trepidation that he was going to tell me off for wearing my tie wonkily, I received some glowing praise and a nice little pay rise as a reward for my efforts over my first six months here. Somehow, I seem to be doing a good job.

So this week, I have taken a week's holiday, and am in the middle of showing Caroline and Anne the sights and sounds of Dubai. They are in their last week here and, other than the impromptu swim in the creek, haven't seen much outside the malls, hotels and our villa. Teresa and I haven't seen much of it either, to be fair, which is why we waited until I was off work to do all the touristy stuff.

A desert safari had always on the cards, so I booked one for Saturday with a company called Arabian Nights Tours. We were told that we would be picked up at just after 3pm on Saturday afternoon. After the usual confusion over our exact location in the maze that is

Springs, (phone rings: "I'm outside your villa", "Er...No you're not", "Er...oops, sorry, wrong street"....) our driver arrived in his shiny silver Toyota Land Cruiser. He was an agreeable gentleman from Tanzania going by the name of Kashmir, and made sure we were all comfortable and well looked after before we left. With all six passengers squeezed into the huge vehicle, we set off from our villa at about 3.30pm, and headed out of town, towards the Hatta road and the desert.

After about forty-five minutes we reached a rendezvous point at a small group of shops and cafés, where a dozens of other Land Cruisers from various tour companies were gathering. Kashmir told us that we had a few minutes to visit the shops and answer the call of nature and so on, so I took it as an opportunity to get some drinks. I was invited to buy all manner of trinkets and foodstuffs and drinks by the many shopkeepers stood around, and by the time I left, I had a new hat, three cans of "Bebsi" and a bagful of goodies for the rest of the journey.

We ended up staying at the rendezvous point for a good twenty minutes. By the time we set off again, there must have been thirty of the giant 4x4s parked in front of the shops. The Arabian Nights group set off as one, executing a swift U-turn before turning off the main road onto a smaller provincial road, then turning onto the sand itself. We were treated to a little taster of dune bashing as the car dipped and weaved around a few small dunes. Not too bad, I thought to myself.

We stopped again, right next to a camel farm, and everyone was ordered out of the cars so the drivers could adjust the air pressures in their tyres for the dune bashing to come. As we milled around and had a peek at the camels in their pens, a man with a camera wandered round, taking what we assumed were still pictures of everyone in their individual groups. There were people from all around the world in the various cars, most of them unaware of what lay ahead. Caroline scooped up a handful of sand and showed me how different it was to that found on the beaches. It was smooth and fine; almost like powder, and it blew off our hands in the slightest breeze.

After a few minutes we all climbed back into the vehicles and set off into the desert for real. A procession of white Land Cruisers in single file headed into the real dunes of the real desert, and we soon realised that this wasn't a game any more. We climbed up enormous dunes and drove along the narrowest of crests at the top before sliding sideways down the other side. There were steep descents and climbs, and the car lurched left and right as it navigated its way through the sand. It wasn't too rough, being on the smooth, fine desert sand, but it was pretty...well, invigorating, I suppose. The "oohs" and "aahs" carried on for a while; Joseph sang songs and basically didn't shut up all the way, while I soon fell silent, trying to swallow my increasing trepidation as the dunes got higher and steeper.

The fear levels increased when we got stuck on the side of a dune, after sliding down sideways from the crest. The wheels just wouldn't move us, and we soon realised why sensible people always come out into the desert in groups of cars, rather than alone. The cars behind stopped and aided our driver, digging his wheels out and barking instructions until we were on our way again. Then Kashmir had problems with a particularly steep dune, taking four attempts to climb it. Sensing my rising panic, he patted my shoulder and laughed. I felt like a right wimp. In the back, Joseph chattered and sang, Anne cackled insanely, Teresa sat bolt-upright with a fixed, macabre grin, and Caroline battled hard to stop herself from puking all down my back.

The quietest, calmest person was Emma, who sat there, nice and secure in her booster seat, as if it was just another ride to a shopping mall. I wouldn't have been surprised if she'd gone to sleep. All the while, we barely noticed that we were getting deeper and deeper into the desert, and all signs of civilisation were disappearing. There were no road signs, no pylons, and no tarmac roads: we were truly in the wild now. The only signs of life we spotted were the other cars and the odd group of camels lazily plodding around on the sand without a care in the world.

Thankfully, just before Joseph's increasingly hysterical singing and squealing had driven me to potentially murderous intent, we stopped and everyone left the cramped confines of their cars again, massaging hands that ached from holding on for dear life. We were able to climb up the nearby dunes and take in the views all around. It was then that I appreciated where we were; high up in the middle of the desert, with no sign of a building all around, and very few signs of vegetation. I had the feeling of magnificent isolation, and almost wished that I had been all alone there to witness it in complete solitude.

Small cartons of water were handed out by the drivers and were quickly consumed before we headed off again. The dunes soon petered out and we were driving along flat, tyre-rutted desert plains. Patches of greenery materialised around us, and I realised we were driving in dry wadi beds, and we couldn't have been far from the camp we were heading for. At least, I hoped not.

We stopped again just as the sun was dipping towards the horizon. A light haze sat above the distant dunes, but the rainbow of colours we were expecting never came. Instead, the sun's disc slowly dulled as it sank, and then disappeared altogether in the light-brown haze, like a bright orange digestive biscuit sinking and dissolving into a cup of tea.

The final leg of our journey took us onto the first tarmac road we had seen for what seemed like miles. It's hard to gauge distance out here. The road was an unfinished one, being built right in the middle of nowhere. Pieces of construction machinery stood idly by the new road, like sleeping robot cattle. We drove along this incomplete road for a short distance, and then veered off into more dunes, round a corner, through a large wooden gate, and finally the camp appeared ahead.

We pulled up and Kashmir turned and smiled at us all knowingly. We all smiled back, glad to be on level land, and piled out of the car. The camp was a fort-styled structure, with wooden walls and towers on each corner. Inside, low Bedouin-style tables and floor cushions waited for the guests. A log fire set in a pit was just starting to catch and a falcon swooped overhead. In one corner the barbeque was smoking away, tended to by three men preparing our feast. In another corner a souvenir shop with gaudy lighting attracted the visitors like moths to a lamp, but the best thing I spied was the little window surrounded by cable lights selling something I was more than ready for - BOOZE.

A cooling, calming bottle of Corona Extra was vanquished in seconds and we sat under the darkening skies of the desert watching a belly dancer twirl and shimmy in the middle of the camp. Men watched admiringly and women shook their heads, and the dancer proceeded to humiliate a procession of tourists by dragging them up for a dance. Been there; done that on more than one occasion on holidays in places like Greece. I'm glad I had the foresight to choose a seat away from the middle.

Then they served the food, and it was actually pretty good. It was hot and tasty and everything else that food should be, but it's always an unknown quantity on these occasions. After eating, a few people decided to have henna tattoos painted on by a very skilful lady sitting in one corner. Teresa had some ornate patterns painted onto her hand and I got a celtic-style band round my upper arm. That's about as close as I get to having a real tattoo. The permanence and the pain of real tattoos don't really make them an attractive proposition to me.

The final piece of entertainment was the screening of a film depicting short clips of everyone in the party taken by the cameraman we had seen earlier at the camel farm. There were also shots from the desert, various landmarks of Dubai and the odd bit of clichéd desert stuff with camels performing belly dances atop dunes and the like. The bright lights of the camp were lowered while the film played, so I finally got a chance to see the much-vaunted starlit sky in the desert. It was definitely clearer, but with all the lights round the camp, I wouldn't call it spectacular. I considered walking away from the camp to get a better view, but very soon the film was over, and we were all offered the chance to buy a copy on DVD before we were called back to our cars.

The drive back home was a relaxed affair. We were all pretty tired, and glad that Kashmir decided against taking us back through the dunes. I don't think it's an option in the dark anyway, and we were soon driving on proper roads heading back to the city and the bright lights of Sheik Zayed Road. Everyone in the car was silent as we floated past the twinkling skyscrapers, and we got home just before 10pm, feeling that we'd had a real adventure.

Wednesday, February 21, 2007

The Tourist Trap

I'm off on holiday / leave / vacation (call it what you will) this week, as I've mentioned, so have been taking the chance to do a few more of the touristy things and take the in-laws to see a few places before they head back to the UK on Friday night. It has certainly been an experience for them. Certain people from work have still managed to call me almost every day. The place is falling apart without me. Well, canteen takings are down, that's for sure.

We spent one of these last few days at a beach resort. It was in the Marina area, and we had to drive through a massive building site (even more of a building site than usual) to get there. The dust was really bad that day, as it was quite windy, and it was even worse around the Marina area, where they are building the massive, monolithic, and frankly ugly towers that make up the Jumeirah Beach Residence. All kinds of trucks, cement mixers and construction plant were whizzing around or parked in stupid places (with the obligatory hazard lights on). We got lost, or should I say misdirected, by poor road signs, but got there eventually.

Once inside the hotel, we made our way to the private beach, paying a one hundred dirham fee for the privilege, of course. But that's OK, because the beach in this place was a world away from the Jumeirah Beach Park. The litter was minimal, and there were free towels, plentiful sun loungers and parasols, as well as good catering facilities.

Nearer the hotel itself there were swimming pools, and between the pools and the beach, there was a patch of lush grass spotted with loungers. Near the end of the beach where we decided to camp ourselves there was a big play area for the little ones, and to one side, near the gentle, turquoise waves of the Gulf, there was a water sports booth, with kayaks, dinghies and giant inflatable bananas available to hire. The best thing about the place was the lack of airborne dust. The beach was quite well sheltered from the elements (apart from the sun, which contrived to burn me, as is its wont).

So we lounged on loungers, paddled in the cool sea, and generally soaked up the chilled holiday atmosphere. After an hour, I hinted heavily at my hunger levels to the wife, so we headed up to the outdoor restaurant by the grass area and had a reasonably good barbeque buffet lunch. I think we were on the menu as well, because Teresa was bitten several times on her legs by something under the table. It must be said, the flies were annoying, and there seems to be increasing numbers of them at this time of year.

After lunch, we moved to the pool area to let the kids have a good splash and play in the kiddie pool, until Emma decided she'd had enough, and filled her swimming nappy with something slightly less pleasant-smelling than a dead rat with a body odour problem. We took that as our cue to leave, but had enjoyed a good few hours there in the sun. My red head and shoulders were testament to that.

On another evening, just as the sun was setting, we went to the Marina promenade area and ate a pleasant al-fresco meal at an Italian restaurant, even though it turned slightly chilly towards the end. As darkness fell, we watched the towers around the Marina light up in their many different colours. Even the cranes light up round here, and I watched them for a while as they beavered away on their unrelenting, 24/7 mission to finish Dubai.

After the meal we walked back towards the large, round water feature on the walkway between the Main towers, and Joseph and Emma took great delight in jumping in and out of the water jets that were set into the pavement as they danced to their pre-set programmes. The kids got soaked, but had good fun. Luckily, Teresa had come prepared with changes of clothing. Caroline chose to abstain from getting wet again.

As the kids played I took a seat at the nearby promenade cafe and ordered a *shisha* and watched the fun. When they'd finished, we all sat down and the *shisha* was passed around. After a bit of the usual spluttering and the odd comical expression, we headed home again.

Today, we decided to go for an Afternoon Tea at a nice hotel. We ended up at the Ritz Carlton, which is also in the Marina area. Once again I managed to get lost, mainly due to those bad signs, or so I told our guests. We had wanted to do the tea thing in the Burj Al Arab, but when we'd phoned them to enquire they told us we weren't nearly posh enough. Or maybe it was because they were fully booked until the end of the month.

Either way, the Ritz Carlton did not disappoint in the slightest. Scones, cakes and sandwiches galore were brought to the table on tiered silver trays, and we polished them off with little moans and exclamations of pleasure. The food really was top notch. The surroundings were superb as well, with massive chandeliers hanging from a dark varnished wood ceiling, giant plush sofas and chairs to sink into, and a lady on the piano in the corner playing a selection of inoffensive background music. Through the windows we could see the Arabian Gulf, looking particularly clear today, with a few white-topped waves rushing in on the landward breeze. Why isn't it always this good?

Tomorrow we're going to go on a Big Bus ride, which is an open-topped bus that tours the city. I will definitely be putting on some sun-block tomorrow, having learned my lesson at the beach.

Saturday, February 24, 2007
Back to life...back to reality

Caroline and Anne are back at home now. I conveyed them to the airport last night to catch their flight. Over their last few days we have really lived it up. We had a super afternoon tea at the Ritz Carlton, then spent Thursday on the Big Bus going round Bur Dubai, under the creek through the Shindaga tunnel and a jaunt around Deira before returning over the Maktoum Bridge. I had to suppress loud guffaws when the tour guides pointed out the various buildings all around us, breathlessly telling us about how some were built nearly *twenty years ago!*

We alighted at the Dubai Museum, which is situated in a proper old building (a rare sight round here) to have a look round, and it was excellent. I had thought it was just a few minor exhibits above ground in the grounds of the old fort it is located in, but there is a huge underground gallery with some fascinating exhibits on Dubai and Bedouin culture. After the museum visit we had lunch in a courtyard café in the "historic" Bastakiya area, which is closely-bunched group of traditional Arabic buildings, all topped with their trademark wind towers. I had a taste of camel meat in a stew, and it wasn't bad - quite like beef, I would say.

That night, Teresa and I took the opportunity to go out on our own, and went to the BiCE restaurant at the Jumeirah Hilton. It was terrific. Great food, superb service and a lovely atmosphere made for a really pleasant evening. A couple of hours of freedom from the kids was just good to have as well. We had a nightcap cocktail in the BiCE skybar on the 10th floor to finish off the night on a sophisticated note. Well, we tried to be sophisticated. Our Yorkshire accents kind of jarred with the whole atmosphere. "Aye, lad. Git us one of them there fancy drinks, pet. A bloody drink called Man'attan? Ee bye gum, ecky thump. That's some backwater over t'pond, in't it?"

So Friday - yesterday - was the last day for our visitors. We had an easy, lazy day, culminating in a drive along the Jumeirah Beach Road to catch the sunset and a final meal out at the Dhow and Anchor in the Jumeirah Beach Hotel. They have a lovely wooden terrace area to sit out and watch the world go by, with views of the nearby Burj Al Arab through the trees. Like with most places round here, the best time to go to them is just before sunset, in my opinion. The light fades quickly, the sky turns into exquisite mix of colours, and then the artificial lights come on all around you. It felt like the last night of a holiday for all of us.

Following the meal of average pub food (all the food I've had at JBH is average standard but not average prices) we wandered down to the waterfront and took in the magnificent views of the Burj Al Arab as the lights shining on the sail changed colour and searchlights on the helicopter pad swayed to and fro, casting long beams into the darkening sky.

On the way out, we saw a paparazzo waiting with his camera poised for some celeb or other, but after a quick call on his mobile, he disappeared in a large car. Our car was delivered to us by the valet, and we bundled in as quickly as we could before driving off amongst all the Hummers, Beamers and other expensive-looking vehicles, filled with expensive-looking women.

An hour or two later, I was on the way to the airport with the in-laws. Joseph came with me while Teresa and Emma stayed at home. Emma was in bed by the time we set off. Caroline and Anne were quiet and contemplative as we sailed along the Sheik Zayed Road, taking in the bright lights of the Marina, the various Burjs and the Trade Centre for one last time.

The traffic thickened up over Garhoud Bridge, but we got there in plenty of time. The airport was a manic multi-coloured muddle of faces preparing to fly all over the globe, dressed in a million different ways, all clutching a bewildering array of luggage, but all united in the common goal of getting ready to fly somewhere.

Caroline and Anne said their goodbyes and melted into the crowds moving through to the departure areas. Joseph and I set off for home, sad that our guests had left, but remembering that we will soon be greeting my own parents and brother very soon. Less than six weeks now, and we'll be doing all this again.

On the way home, I had a bit of a brush with what I will politely call Land Cruiser Man. I came back round the Garhoud way onto Garhoud Bridge, and even at 11pm last night it was ridiculously busy. The road feeds in from the right onto the bridge, and as you approach the bridge, there is a small chevron-painted hard-shoulder area between the driving lane and the wall. As I moved along, a red car pushed in front of me from this area, just in the nick of time. I let it go. Normal standards round here.

Then a white Toyota Land Cruiser with an Abu Dhabi plate pulled alongside. The driver was hidden from view by heavy window tinting, as is the mode with these cars. No chance, thought I; there's not enough room; he would have to drop in behind me.

But this one had other ideas. He (I assumed it was a he) was utterly *determined* to get ahead of me. He obviously needed those extra few seconds and also had to show the foreigner who was boss.

I wasn't about to be bullied, so kept moving, thinking that he had to give in. But then he dived across the front of me, clipping my wing mirror as he passed, which flipped his own mirror to the flattened position against the side of his door.

I was utterly astounded. Flabbergasted, astonished, and fucking angry. As we crossed the bridge in the heavy traffic, his car was just in front of me all the way, and he had gained all of two seconds through his arrogant, reckless actions. I think he was hovering in front of me hoping that I'd give him the bird. I kept my hands down, even if I swore quite a lot. I wasn't about to give him an excuse to turn me into the wrong-doer here. Joseph slept through all of this, though he admitted later that he had heard my astonished swearing at Land Cruiser Man and had just hugged his teddy bear a little tighter. I will know who is to blame when that bear starts swearing.

Today, the house feels empty. We went food shopping and just kind of floated around without having much to say to each other. Tomorrow I am back at work and Joseph is back at school. Good old routine. My diet needs it, I can tell you.

Sunday, February 25, 2007
The UAE Highway Code

Someone (rather cheekily, I thought) wrote in to 7 Days and asked if there was a Highway Code for the UAE. I've had a quick go at writing one. Tongue firmly in cheek, of course...

The UAE Highway Code

1: Vehicle condition

You MUST ensure your vehicle and trailer can at least move, whether using motor, camel or donkey traction. Wheels would be nice too. If you are driving a Heavy Goods Vehicle, be sure to adorn it with coloured lights. This might help make you more visible, especially as the vehicle's proper lights don't seem to work.

2: Before setting off

You should ensure that:

- you have kind of planned your route and only allowed enough time to get to your destination if you travel at just under light speed. With a tail wind.

- clothing and footwear are from Harvey Nich's

- you sort of know where all the controls are but have no idea what they do.

- your seat are adjusted correctly to ensure comfort, at least partial control and maybe, just a little bit of good vision. Don't worry about the blacked-out windows. Position the mirror for optimum self-admiring glances.

- head restraints are properly adjusted to reduce the risk of neck injuries in the event of an seeing an attractive woman

- you have sufficient fuel before commencing your journey, especially if it includes motorway driving. The car might only make 50km on one tank, so be careful.

3: Seat Belts

Drivers in the front seat: That black strap thing might look a bit silly across your nice designer clothes, and may even crumple them. It also restricts the driver's movement to the other seat, to the rear of the vehicle to get your CDs, or out of the sunroof. Don't bother. Children aged 3 and under should be restrained by bouncing them on the knee of a passenger, or even the driver, depending on your mood. Hanging them out of the window at 140kph is a good laugh. Children aged 3 to 12 should sit on the roof.

4: Signals

Signals are made with that stick thing behind the steering wheel. Pull it towards you to make people move out of the way. In combination with the horn, this is the only signalling you require.

There are these things called indicators as well, but they only cause confusion and actually, it isn't anyone else's business where you are going.

You should also:

- watch out for hand signals given by other road users and ring the police immediately if they give you the bird.
- Watch for other drivers using indicators. If you see them doing so, you should speed up to prevent them from manoeuvring.
- You SHOULD REALLY obey signals given by police officers and signs used by school crossing patrols. Aw, go on

5: Traffic light signals and traffic signs

Traffic lights are simple. Green means go very fast. Amber means go even faster. Red means go really, really fast, unless the idiot in front has stopped for some reason. As soon as the lights go green again, give the driver in front 3.5 nanoseconds to move before honking angrily and at length.

Traffic signs are there to be knocked over and will probably send you in the wrong direction or give you incorrect information anyway.

6: Flashing headlights

Only flash your headlights in an attempt to intimidate other road users. Do not flash your headlights to let other road users know that you are there.

If another driver flashes his headlights MOVE OUT OF THE WAY IMMEDIATELY. This rule does not apply to White Nissan Sunnys.

7: Hazard warning lights

These marvellous thingies are great for telling other road users that you are a moron. Switch them on when it gets foggy or when it rains in order to remind other road users of what they are already painfully aware of, and keep them guessing as to where you might be going. Everyone else on the road with a brain is more nervous than usual, but that's a good thing. It galvanises the senses.

Also use your hazard warning lights when you need to inexplicably stop in the road and obstruct all other road users.

8: Speed Limits

HA HA HA HA HA HA HA HA!

Ahem.

HA HA HA HA HA HA HA HA HA!

Please ensure you laugh as loud as possible to drown out the annoying chime of the overspeed warning emanating from the dashboard.

9: Lines and Markings on the Road

They look nice, don't they? Give a bit of symmetry to the roads and roundabouts. Anyway, Yellow lines are to be crossed whenever possible. Chevrons painted in an area designate taking-over and pushing-in points for large 4x4 vehicles.

10: Mobile Phones and other technology

Mobile phones are compulsory. They should be stuck to one ear at all times. You might want to keep one hand free for smoking, shaving, applying make-up, reading or selecting a play-list on your I-pod.

11: Overtaking

You MUST get to your destination before everyone else. Don't let Dastardly and Mutley win. End of. Only move away from the fast lane 5 metres before your turn off. Without indicating, naturally.

12: Being Overtaken

I know. It's a mad concept, but it might just happen when you're coming onto a fast road. Don't worry, you'll be in the fast lane soon. Anyway, should anyone in the lane beside you put on their indicator, it means they want you to get closer to the car in front as quickly as possible.

13: Pedestrian Crossings

You're having a laugh, aren't you? Those zebra-patterned things? Nah! If you see anyone stop at them, refer to the last part of the instructions for traffic lights. Anyway, watch out for men in night-shirts running across highways. They could well give your car a nasty dent.

14: Cyclists

Cyclists will come the wrong way down a highway towards you, wobbling around with the weight of whatever it is they have in the huge baskets. They particularly like doing this at night. Without lights.

MARCH

Sunday, March 04, 2007

A week is a long time...

in politics, even more so for office politics. So much can change from day to day and week to week.

Last week, I was buzzing. I was on a real high, heading back to work after my week's break with a pay rise under my belt and the praise of clients and bosses ringing loudly in my ears. I was enjoying my job for the first time in years and the future was brighter than the desert sun.

Soon enough, things turned sour. Things had been going too well. I should have bloody known. One stupid little bloody thing (I won't bore you with the detail) had been forgotten about by both me and a chap who works in our office in Doha (who was also on leave last week) and this gave some people the excuse they needed to knock me off my pedestal with a nonchalant swipe. They then took great pleasure in jumping up and down on the broken pieces like a peeved elephant. One day you're the pigeon; the next day you're the statue covered in cack, wishing you had a gun. The upshot was that work became a tad uncomfortable for a few days towards the end of last week, and I was no longer flavour of the month. When the invite came, I took the opportunity to go for a drink with a mate to let of some steam and drown my sorrows in a few of the more curious bars around Dubai.

Which brings me nicely on to the next subject for today's incoherent rant: We went to a bar called Scarlett's at the Emirates Towers. It's a pleasant enough joint as joints go, and I've been there before with work colleagues. We met some of my mate's friends, and one of them was a young Emirati, who wore a natty black dish-dash and a smart red and white *keffiyeh,* worn in the style of a sort of loose turban, as is fashionable amongst the younger generations. He sat with us sipping Bacardi Breezers quite happily and came across as an urbane and chilled-out kind of guy with a wise head on young shoulders. Of course, Muslims aren't meant to drink alcohol, but they do. I'm not meant to think about sex all day, but I do. Shit, as everyone knows, happens.

But anyway, we were there integrating and getting along famously until a man approached our table. He was dressed like all these hospitality industry managers are, with a cheap navy suit and greased-back hair, exuding self-importance and bristling with truculence. He talked to our local friend in Arabic for a moment, and then disappeared from the scene, returning to pushing his pens and worthing his jobs. Our friend just smiled and casually informed the rest of us that he had been asked to leave the bar by 10pm. I was quite astonished. Here he was, in his own country, and he was being asked to leave an establishment because of who he was and what he was wearing.

Immediately I imagined the uproar if such a thing was to happen in the UK. The right-wing tabloids would have a meadow, pasture and field day, but it didn't bother our Arab friend. He just shrugged it off, finished his drink and left. It wasn't long before the rest of us left to find another bar.

So on Thursday I was a little jaded, but not really too hung over. I'm just glad I'm not a heavy drinker like some of the messes I regularly encounter here. The expat community seems to have a disproportionate number of alcoholics, for some reason. I honestly don't know how they afford it, because booze really isn't that cheap here.

The weekend couldn't have come quick enough. The boss still had time to have a little shout at me for something trivial before letting me go on Thursday night, before which I had managed to get lost going to a meeting in Deira. I finally got to my meeting fifty minutes late, after another session of head-butting the steering wheel and angry assertions to the empty car about how much I hated this place. Hate is a strong word, but that's the red mist for you.

At least ten of those minutes were wasted after I had actually arrived at the office where the meeting was. I spent what seemed like an age trying to get a lift in the most convoluted and absurd lift lobby known to man. Instead of the usual panel of buttons to choose the floor you want inside each lift, there was a console in the middle of the lift lobby which you had to approach and press the number corresponding to the floor you wanted. It then indicated which lift of the four available to use, but I waited an insanely long time for my lift to arrive, whilst other lifts came and went from the ground floor, apparently unable or unwilling to stop at multiple floors in the same trip. I only wanted to get the first floor, but had no idea where the stairs could be; if indeed they existed.

At least Thursday night was relaxing. Teresa went out with some friends and left me alone to watch a DVD or two. I had bought a few from the Chinese lady who comes round the office every week or two, but I only ended up watching one before getting tired and going to bed.

At the weekend we ended up going to the newest shopping mall in town: Festival City. I think Vegetable City sounds better, personally, and it is actually shaped like a cucumber, which is nice. Half the shops aren't open yet; you can't walk along the heavily-featured canal yet, and to be frank, the standard of finish in the sections that have been opened is shockingly bad. They didn't even bother to clean the veneered wood panelling properly, so it looks a bit dusty. What do we say? It'll be nice when it's finished...

Sunday, March 11, 2007
Hi Ho, Hi Ho, it's off to Doha again...

It's been a tiring weekend. I'll tell you more about it when I get back from Doha on Monday night.

Update: Got to the airport this morning and was bumped off my early morning Emirates flight to the early afternoon one. Ho-hum. The nice Emirates man said it was really busy today and they had loads of people being bumped. I suppose that's the risk when they over-book the flights.

So, while I'm waiting to go back to the airport, I can expand on the weekend.

Yesterday we decided to try the Dreamland Aqua Park over in Umm Al Qwain (sorry if that's not the right spelling). We've already done Wild Wadi, and a friend of mine, Martin (who I met in my first few weeks in Dubai), has repeatedly told me it is nicer at Dreamland. More pleasant, much cheaper, and best of all in his opinion: they sell alcohol on the premises.

So on Saturday morning we set off, with Martin and his son, Liam, coming along for the ride. We headed along the Emirates Road, passing through the delights of Sharjah and Ajman on the way, and after an hour or so we arrived at Dreamland, situated as it is right next to a lagoon.

You know you're just about there when you see a huge, ancient Russian cargo plane casually abandoned by the side of the road. I looked for POLICE ARE AWARE stickers, but I don't think they could reach the windscreen. Joseph and Liam spent the whole journey annoying each other and the other passengers with dog impressions, pillow fights and truck-spotting contests, so it was relief to arrive and emerge from the car into the warm sunshine.

In the park itself, it soon became apparent why it was cheaper than Wild Wadi. It was much, much older, and it showed. The metal grates in some of the pools were spotted with rust, the grout in between the tiles was somewhat grubby and the slides and other apparatus all around the park were faded and worn. On the other hand it was a more pleasant area than Wild Wadi; much more spread out with large green lawns, plenty of trees to shelter under and loads of loungers to soak up the sunshine on. It was also much quieter, with hardly any queues for even the major rides.

After a short play in the kiddies' pool we had a lunch of cheap and nasty fast food, and then Martin and I tried and failed to persuade our boys to join us in riding on anything higher than six feet off the ground. We tried bribery, blackmail, threats and just general cajoling, but to no avail.

Joseph even climbed up a steep slope with me to the entrance of a ride named the Black Hole. I knew he wasn't keen, but he was hoping to get a large ice cream as a reward afterwards. He finally cracked at the sight of the pitch-dark tunnel. His soft whimpering turned into full-scale screaming and crying and without any masking tape to hand, we had to come back down the stairs past people wearing smug, knowing smiles.

In the end, us men had a few goes on the big slides by ourselves, but soon tired of walking half a mile up a slope and some stairs to reach a ride that lasted all of ten seconds, and which invariably resulted in swimming shorts having to be surgically extracted from bum cracks.

With the day drawing on, we decided to leave. Joseph and Liam had a short session in the tatty, half-closed video arcade, playing a best-of-three round of air hockey, which my son won. GET IN! Not that I'm competitive or anything, you understand.

We left Dreamland behind and drove round the corner to the more adult-orientated attraction which everyone in Dubai talks of in fond, often misty-eyed terms: Barracuda. Barracuda is basically an off-licence / alcohol outlet, but the attraction is that it sells tax-free alcohol and you don't need to produce a liquor licence.

It's a useful place to go when you need to stock up, so that's what I did. With more visitors due to arrive in less than four weeks, I used it as an excuse to go on a trolley dash round the spirits and wine section and equip myself with a half-decent drinks selection, including gin, whisky, vodka, Bacardi, Baileys and a few bottles of wine. The trolley-full of booze I left with cost me seven hundred dirhams, or about a hundred quid. It would probably have cost nearly twice as much from an MMI or A&E in Dubai (the latter is a great name for a booze shop, by the way).

Then we drove through Sharjah, the dry Emirate, at quite a pace, although not too fast in case we attracted police attention. I have heard scare stories about people being crashed into – on purpose – and blackmailed by dodgy types who look out for heavily-laden cars carrying Westerners and booze. I don't think there's really a problem, it's probably one of those scare stories / urban legends that people like to frighten naive newcomers with, but it is technically illegal to have booze there, or even transport it through the emirate. Then again, Sharjah airport has a Duty Free section. Work that one out. Consistency? I don't think there's actually a Gulf Arabic word for it.

On the way home we stopped off at the Irish Village, a Dubai expat institution near the airport, where a couple of pints of the black stuff and a bit of stodgy food rounded off the day. It's quite an agreeable location, with a lake, a children's play area and a massive terrace on which one can sit and watch the world go by. It's situated right in the heart of Garhoud, and is a bit of an oasis in the city. The standard pub food comes quickly, the bar staff are either surly or deaf, but it's popular and pleasant enough.

Well, that's the time used up. I'd better make my way back to the airport.

Wednesday, March 14, 2007
Hazy Daze in Doha

Doha: I still struggle with the correct pronunciation of the name. I sometimes say, "Dough-wuh," but then hear someone else say, "Doh-Hah", giving much more emphasis to the second syllable. One of them is right, I guess.

I got there eventually. I had already checked in on the morning after being bumped onto the afternoon flight, so I just stopped by check-in to find out the gate number before proceeding through passport control.

Now that I have a residence visa stamped in my passport, I had the pleasure of using the e-gate system for the first time, and even though I managed to cock it up by forgetting which finger I was meant to scan, I got through fairly quickly. It is a fantastic system. You scan your card on a reader at the first electronic gate, which is a bit like the barriers in the London Underground, then when it opens with a Star-Trek style swish, you move into the next section where you are instructed to scan your finger on the infra-red reader. Finally (if you use the right finger) it bleeps and opens the next gate and you are through, laughing and pointing at the sad sacks queuing to get their passports stamped. It's even better on the way back in. You can be out of the airport in fifteen minutes if you don't have any baggage checked.

The plane ride was a bit of a bumpy one. The crew gave us our snacks of roasted vegetable sandwiches and Arabic sweets just after take-off before snatching them back as we took the first bite. It is a short flight, admittedly and they must have known we were likely to hit turbulence, and we did, especially as we approached to land in Doha. As ever in these situations, I planted my feet firmly on the floor and gripped the chair arms tightly, which would surely help if something disastrous happen.

We managed to land safely and I was lucky enough to find a shuttle bus for my hotel waiting outside, so took the opportunity to check in at the hotel before heading over to my company's offices. Within an hour we were having a long meeting about the Big Hole in the Ground with people from the company assigned the lovely task of building something nice in the Big Hole. It went quite well; well enough for us all to remain on talking terms, which is always a bonus, and then it was home time. It was decided that a few of us would head out to watch the England v France rugby game in a bar called Aussie Legends in the Rydges Plaza Hotel. I went back to the hotel first to freshen up before joining the others in the bar.

Aussie Legends is one of those typical expat bars, full of large televisions and chain-smoking antipodeans. A couple of nice pints of Guinness were consumed while we watched the English rugby team pull out all the stops to beat the French. It was a good atmosphere, without the slightest hint of bother even bubbling under. The only annoyance was a large, hairy man of unknown nationality (but definitely not English) who shouted, "WAHEY" every time France had the ball near the try line or when England made a mistake. His braying soon quietened towards the end of the match as England romped home for a comfortable win.

After the rugby we headed down to the Italian restaurant on the Ground Floor (the scene of an interesting political discussion on a previous visit) and ate a pleasant, if unspectacular meal, chewing the fat in decent company for a good couple of hours. My early start again caught up with me. I was almost falling asleep at the table and I was glad to get back to my hotel for some kip.

Monday morning, and after a bit of room service breakfast I made my way over to the office, from where we drove over to the site on the Corniche. As we drove along the Corniche, with the sun shining down on the city, I again noticed what a pleasing-on-the-eye place Doha can be. There aren't many cranes, but there are loads of palm trees lining the roads and expanses of grass everywhere, and the buildings are nicely spread out.

The Corniche itself is a large sweeping C-shape, with a small, deserted island in the middle of the bay, which allegedly used to be home to a restaurant at one time. At one end of the big C is the airport and sea port, and at the other end you can see the beginnings of a Sheik Zayed Road-style skyscraper zone, with gleaming new buildings rising along the shoreline. Past that is the new Pearl Island, which sounds like an impressive development, built in the shape of a string of pearls. There is little doubt that they are copying Dubai in some respects, but like I said before, I hope they don't try too hard. The place has a real Middle-Eastern identity and feel to it that should be retained so it offers something different from Dubai. I get the impressions they are trying to strike something of a balance. One major difference with Dubai is that the bulk of the work here is commercial and centred around oil and gas rather than tourism.

We arrived at and entered the site complex, walking along the precariously-balanced scaffolding walkway along the front of the cabins that are perched on the side of the Big Hole in the Ground. The Hole was a hive of activity, with cranes and piling rigs and all other manner of machines banging, digging and grinding away. The noise was reaching ear-splitting levels, and the narrow scaffolding walkway beneath us shuddered and vibrated unnervingly as we inched along towards the cabins that overlook the site.

We met with the client's Project Manager in his office, and even with the door shut the racket from outside was obtrusive. The PM glumly admitted that he would often leave the site and find somewhere else to work just to get some peace and quiet. He soon perked up when he remembered the news from Dubai. He cheerily told us that there had been an accident at Dubai Airport this morning, where a Bangladesh Airlines plane had failed to take off and had slid off the runway. The airport was therefore closed and all flights to and from Dubai were cancelled. Once again, it looked like I would be staying in Doha for longer than anticipated. It seems I either struggle to get to Doha or away from the place; never in between.

We still had to go through with the site progress meeting, half of which I missed due to the constant noise of banging and digging outside. The other half passed right over my head as engineers talked technical jargon that may have well been in Martian. I should record these meetings for when I have insomnia. The worst bit is, whenever I am right on the verge of slumber, or daydreaming about dancing hippos being hunted by panthers in smoking jackets, someone will turn to me and ask my opinion. Er... is it something to do with debonair big cats? No? Let me get back to you on that one.

Actually, I do wake up when I'm needed, pretty much always towards the end of the meetings, when they deem it appropriate to talk about commercial matters, or how much money it's costing to make a lot of noise with over-sized Tonka toys in a Big Bloody Hole in the Ground. And invariably, it's costing too much and I have to tell them why.

Somehow I managed to blag it once again and after the meeting adjourned we returned to our offices. The secretary told me that the problems at Dubai had been sorted out and there were now flights available back to Dubai. My original 2.25pm was now scheduled to take off at 3.30pm, so I procured a lift to the airport, checked in, passed through passport control and had a quick browse in Duty Free.

As I was looking at something to buy the kids, there was an electronic *bing-bong* from the public address system. As always, the Arabic version of the announcement was first, but my ears pricked up when I heard my airline's name (out of kindness, and to protect the innocent, I will call them BLOODY EMIRATES) in amongst the husky tones and throat-clearing noises of the announcement. Then came the English version, and the words, "We regret to inform you that..." told me all I needed to know. My flight was cancelled.

Bugger.

There I was, stuck in limbo, with my passport still freshly adorned with an exit stamp and a boarding pass. I asked an official-looking lady milling around near passport control what was going on and what we should do, and they said she would ask before hurrying off somewhere. The departure information screen showed the words CANCELLED in large white letters next to my flight.

Bugger times two.

The official-looking woman returned and said that a representative of BLOODY EMIRATES would come through to update us in a few minutes. A couple of other people had joined me by now, looking at their watches impatiently, shaking their heads and looking back up at the information board in case it changed. We were told to wait by the gate, but then the *bing-bong* sounded again, telling us that the flight was just delayed. The board still said CANCELLED. Confusion abounded, but most of us decided to wait by the gate for someone to come and tell us what the heck was going on.

It was a long wait. No-one from BLOODY EMIRATES appeared. It transpired that seventy people had been allowed to check in before the flight had been cancelled. Mobile phones were hammered by people ringing home, the office, the airline or even their dog, who would probably have been of infinitely more use than BLOODY EMIRATES.

In the process of making enquiries, I found out that the airline's Doha operation actually closes for three hours in the afternoon. How very professional of them. I rang the Dubai branch and was told that our flight was definitely off. The next one was at 11.15pm.

Bugger squared.

Someone then piped up with the quite startling information that Doha International Airport actually closes between 3pm and 7pm every single day for maintenance or goose chasing or something like that.

Bugger cubed, Bollocks and For Fuck's Sake!

I rang our Doha office to tell them about the situation, but with no-one having any real knowledge of what to do in this situation (could we just go out through passport control again?) there wasn't really much to be said. After a little bit more waiting, a sheepish man shuffled towards us (not from BLOODY EMIRATES, surprisingly) and said we could go upstairs to the café and have a complimentary sandwich and drink. Information would have been nice, but that wasn't on the menu, apparently. We just had to wait and eat snacks.

As it was, no-one from BLOODY EMIRATES showed up to tell anyone anything. I only found out what I had to do because I spotted the lady (airport employee, non-airline affiliated) who had checked me in sitting in the café. She told me to go to the Transfer Desk. Why couldn't someone have told us that before? Where was the announcement? It seems that the message had been spreading by word-of-mouth, and by the time I reach the Transfer Desk, a gaggle of tired, confused passengers was gathered there, waving boarding passes and pleading for some news. We were all offered passes to the Business Class Lounge and a seat on the 11.15pm. Marvellous, thought I. An eight-hour wait for a plane that may not even leave.

I could have taken them up on this offer and drunk the Business Class Lounge bar dry, but thought better of it and asked if I could come back the next day instead. I was told I could, and instructed to leave through the arrivals section by passing through the Transfer security section back into immigration and having my exit stamp cancelled.

That I did, walking through an eerily deserted passport control manned by one official then past static, empty luggage carousels and out into the open air again. There weren't any planes arriving *or* leaving, it appeared. I rang our Doha office to tell them to book me a hotel room for the night then caught a cab to the office and browsed the internet for what was left of the working day.

The Doha office manager was receptive to the idea of having a beer and a bite that night, so we took off at 6pm and had a very pleasant evening eating a seafood buffet at my hotel. We got on very well, and the seeds of something were planted that night. I mean that future plans were considered, nothing pervy.

I have been working in Dubai on a project taking place in Doha since I arrived in August last year, and aside from the odd blip, have done a good job, or so I'm told. Personally, I feel like I've half-blagged it, but then the job is as much about being able to hold your own in negotiations and confrontations. It's about saying the right things at the right times to the right people, and being able to do a few pretty spreadsheets on MS Excel.

Whatever; I know what I mean. The possibility of me moving to Doha, either alone on a weekly basis, or with the family in tow, has now entered my mind as an option. The people in Doha seem to be keen to get me there on a permanent basis, even if the people in Dubai would probably not want to lose me (they've said as much). I know the job and I know the people on the job, I wouldn't actually be changing companies, and honestly I would like to see the job through to its end. I would like to see this ninety-storey tower sparkling in the sunlight of the Arabian Gulf where there used to be a Big Hole in the Ground. I've seen the drawings; now I want to see the reality, even if I'll have to take some tranquilisers before even thinking about going up in a lift to the top of the finished building.

There's more to it than just a fear of heights. The original foundations contractor had their contract terminated after putting in some particularly shoddy work. There were even allegations that they falsified their concrete test results. When it comes to the foundations for such a high building, there is little excuse for such shenanigans, and hearing things like this just makes me even more nervous about climbing anything higher than ten storeys in this region.

But back to Doha itself. Of course, I realise that I have previously expressed doubts about Doha as a place to live, but it's grown on me. Dubai is great in its own way. It has the bright lights, the malls, the hotels and all that. It also has things like traffic and hassle and maddeningly conspicuous consumption that just jar with my personal outlook, not to mention the whole issue of class and inherent racism.

It's also a very cliquey, shallow kind of place. I've heard it said that it's like Hong Kong, where it's difficult to make friends amongst the numerous established expats who have lived there for years and like to stick to their closed circles of friends. I also think it's more suited to the single person than a family man.

Bahrain and Qatar are more family-friendly, some have said. Doha may be a small place, with less in the way of tourist attractions, but it is quieter, calmer, less materialistic, it has far less traffic and isn't far from Dubai if you do fancy a mad weekend in the Vegas of the Middle East.

It's a real quandary. Teresa and the kids are settling in. They've made a few friends. I think they like it here. Well most of it. Even though it's all this is just idle speculation at the moment, I've got a lot of thinking to do.

Knowing me, I'll feel completely different tomorrow, and after another weekend of eating out in great locations and having a good time with my family, I might never want to leave. Who knows?

I did finally get back to Dubai on Tuesday, and the flight was only half an hour late this time.

Monday, March 19, 2007
Southgate's Cat

The weather has been acting strangely this last week. We had sandstorms for a couple of days, which meant driving round wasn't as pleasurable as it can be (if the traffic isn't too bad, that is). All the familiar sights were obscured by the sand in the air as we drove past them, with the ghostly shadow of the familiar landmarks just visible through a coffee-creamy murk. Walking from the car to any building involved adopting a troubled, twisted expression, with mouth firmly shut to stop any sand getting in.

After the sandstorms and the increasing humidity, we had a short burst of thunder storms on Saturday night. The thunder storms can be quite impressive here. We saw several awe-inspiring examples of fork lightning as we returned from a meal at Ibn Batutta mall. The storm passed overhead very quickly at about midnight, and sprinkled some rain on us. This was most annoying as I had taken the time to hose my car down to rid it of the thick layer of sand left by the sandstorms, and when it rains here, our partially-covered, slatted-roofed carport spills more sand onto the cars. We are constantly fighting a losing battle with sand in this place.

At least the storms took the humidity away. It was much fresher on Sunday as I headed back to work after another all-too-brief weekend. The airborne sand was also gone, and the familiar sights of towers, cranes and more cranes were visible once more. A stiff breeze was still blowing, though, and on the roads, ribbons of fine sand rippled across the tarmac like ghostly snakes coming back to claim the desert from all this maddening development.

I've been feeling shite again as well. The dust and sand are playing havoc with my sinuses, and I've been feeling just generally bad, even dizzy at times. I had to turn down a friend's invitation to visit the mountains and *wadis* near Hatta over the weekend, and decided to see the doctor on Friday. I was soon laid there on the surgery bed, submitting myself to his probing and prodding, waiting for the verdict. After a moment he stepped away from me, straightened up and sighed.

"How old are you?" he asked sharply.

"Er...Thirty six," said I, almost apologetically.

"And you have *so* many diseases!" he said, shaking his head.

I had no real answer to that.

Turns out I had a sinus infection. Yes, I am a wreck. What can I tell you? I've been through it all before; the dodgy ticker, the shagged hip, the sinuses, the things I won't mention... I'm a walking medical text book, and a hypochondriac to boot. They call it *cyber*chondria these days, because people like me spend hours looking up symptoms and diseases on the internet at the slightest twinge. I think I've worked my way up to "T" in the medical dictionary. There's definitely some ringing in my ears.

It would be great to wake up and have a day when I didn't feel rotten. I can't remember how that feels. I can only hope. Enough, enough! I'll be setting of down that path of self-pity again, and that's half the problem, I reckon, so onwards and sideward we go.

If you haven't yet given up on this entry / chapter, you're probably wondering what the title "Southgate's Cat" refers to. If you're not, look away now and get yourself a cup of tea. I may have mentioned before that I am a follow of Middlesbrough Football Club. I'm a glory supporter through and through, I admit it. Still, being an exiled fan is something of a unique experience. I remember being in the USA in 1998 and having to listen to BBC World Service on my short-wave radio for snippets of news about the team. The only games I saw on TV were the FA Cup Final between Arsenal and Newcastle and some World Cup games. With the time difference, they often kicked off at 9am, which meant an early start in the pub.

Nowadays, English football benefits from blanket TV coverage all over the world and every weekend expat bars around the globe fill with supporters of various English Premier League teams hoping to see their team win. There are a few bars in Dubai that show every single game that is on, thanks to having wall-to-wall TV screens. I've been in a few of them, and it can be difficult to concentrate on one game with all the others going on around you, especially when people in various replica shirts jump up and cheer a goal in the game they're watching, and you turn back in time to see that you've just missed a goal in the game *you* were watching.

Of course, weekend games are the best, because they usually kick off at 6pm or 7pm here depending on the BST/GMT situation in the UK. Sunday games are sometimes a little later, but it's quite nice being able to go out for a drink on an evening and catch a game. Then there are the midweek games which invariably kick off at 7.45 or 8.00pm in the UK. If you're a die-hard, hardcore fan (read NUTTER, but each to their own...you NUTTER), that's OK, you just stay up till 2am to watch the game. That isn't for me. I have enough problems with lack of quality sleep as it is, so I'm not really keen on staying up to watch late matches, especially on a school night.

The problem with this is that I've missed all the cup replays this season, because they are invariably played on Tuesday or Wednesday nights. Boro have contrived to get all the way to the Quarter Finals of the FA Cup this season, and have just happened to need replays in the last three rounds. That's all of them, I think: Hull, Bristol City and West Brom. We've also had to win two penalty shoot-outs to get here.

As fate has it, we drew with Manchester United just over a week ago, and need to go to a replay at Old Trafford (We might as well not turn up, if I'm honest, but you never know). Every time there is a Boro game like this I go to bed at the normal time and the game is played as I sleep. In the morning I wake up completely oblivious to the result of the game until I get downstairs and switch on Sky News just in time for the sports bulletin. In the period between waking up and watching the report, as far as I'm concerned, anything could have happened. Boro could have won gloriously, lost heavily, won on penalties, or just decided to forgo the game at the last minute and go shopping for manbags at the Trafford Centre. I really don't know, and until I see the result on the news, all the possibilities still exist; well for me at least. Tonight, I will be going through this again, even though in my heart I know Boro have about as much chance of surviving as a sausage roll at a Meatloaf after-gig party.

Now this phenomenon of multiple, simultaneous possibilities is what those boffin types refer to as the many-worlds interpretation or MWI (also known as *relative state formulation, theory of the universal wave function, many-universes interpretation, Oxford interpretation* or *many worlds*). It's all to do with quantum mechanics, apparently. A clever Austrian physicist chap called Erwin Schrödinger came up with a theoretical experiment involving a cat locked in a box with a vial of poisonous gas that had a fifty percent chance of being released by a switch connected to a Geiger counter which is placed near some decaying radioactive substance of indeterminate type.

Still with me?

Until the box is opened, no-one knows whether the cat is alive or dead. It is in a state of flux, and both states (dead and alive) exist at the same time. There is also some guff about the interference of the observer and whether it has any influence on the result, and how there could be an infinite number of universes (multiverses) based on all possible outcomes of all situations that have happened, EVER. Then, as someone else has pointed out (Terry Pratchett, I believe), the boffins never considered the possibility of a third state: Bloody Furious Cat.

So, there you have it: this situation could be called Southgate's Cat, in honour of our new rookie manager. If Boro win tonight, the cat will live. If they lose, the cat will be sent to the nearest labour camp. If you believe the papers, it will soon become dinner for the poor, starving labourers.

(Don't worry, there isn't really a cat. I'm off to give my brain a rest now.)

Tuesday, March 20, 2007
The Cat...

is dead. On opening the "box" this morning, I found out that Boro had lost to another dodgy penalty awarded to Man U. The dream is over for another season. I think meeting Paul Scholes (who was suspended for the game) coming out of one of the hotels at the Madinat should have been taken as an omen of impending doom. His mock sympathy at my admission of being a Boro fan was a bloody cheek, mind.

So I stuck a picture of Cristiano Ronaldo's face on the cat and sent it to the nearest labour camp. I hope they like Portuguese.

Sunday, March 25, 2007
A Bridge Over Troubled Wadis

Being the sad bastard with techy/geeky, almost anorak-wearing tendencies that I am, I thought it would be nice for us to have a drive over the new bridge over the creek that opened a couple of weeks ago. It seems to have been given the honour of being given two names, which can lead to some confusion on the approach to it. In most of the blurb that was faithfully trotted out in the local press, along with promises of improved traffic flow, ease of access and free camel cheese, it was named "The Ras Al Khor" bridge, by virtue of it's proximity to that oasis of verdant nature inhabited by long-legged, pink birds. Fair enough.

And then the bridge opened. One morning the Oud Metha Road had magically sprouted a two-lane branch and a set of traffic lights. A yellow sign with the smallest words I have ever seen printed on a road sign (obviously designed by an optician) informed the confused drivers who were hurtling merrily along that they could fork left to go to Dubai or bear right to go over the new bridge. It was a bit messy those first few days while people got used to which lane they were meant to be in, and then they reverted to their usual tactic of switching lanes at the last possible second.

As the days progressed, more signs appeared around Dubai, but most of them were directing the drivers to the "Business Bay Crossing". It sort of points towards the huge Business Bay development, but isn't really that close to it at all, but there we go.

Who am I to argue? I mean, that's not the name the press were giving, but then the local press print stories that the Brother Grimm would be proud of. There is no crime whatsoever in Dubai! All labourers are happy in their work! Riiiiight.

Back to the bridge...I can imagine a few people get confused by this situation as they weave along in their Nissan Sunny at a leisurely pace, faithfully following the signs for Business Bay Crossing. All of a sudden, the signs disappear, and they are faced with a sign pointing to Ras Al Khor Bridge. I bet they go completely crazy and drive into the creek, sending flamingos flying.

I went crazy, but not because of the signs. I went crazy because I assumed (wrongly) that the new bridge would take me right up to the entrance of Festival City, thereby rendering Garhoud Bridge a redundant piece of civil engineering. As we drove over the bridge, everything looked fine. It wasn't actually complete yet; it's a double bridge with six lanes each side, and only one side was open so far. The main thing was that it went over the creek, and was free of queues of impatient drivers with twitchy horn fingers.

The problem became apparent as we came down onto the far shore. As we started coming down at the other end of the bridge we could see Festival City, but as the road from the bridge filtered towards and then joined the main road, we watched helplessly as the exit to Festival City passed us by in a blur. The road from the bridge merged with the main road about fifty yards too late.

This is life in Dubai: You can see what you want, but you can't have it. You'd have thought they'd have built the bridge so you could get straight into Festival City. Oh, no. That would be far too simple. So, as is the custom here, we ended up driving in a huge, ten kilometre loop to get back to the Festival City exit. This is infrastructure planning of stunning proportions. Had I been a local, of course, I would have just driven the wrong way up the main road or reversed for fifty yards to get to the exit. By the time we reached the car park under Marks and Spencers I was frothing like a badly-pulled pint.

I calmed down after some retail therapy and a cup of coffee, and despite Teresa insisting on a visit to the Plastic Swedish Hell we all know as IKEA, I left Festival City in a reasonable mood. I thought about trying to get back over the creek on the new bridge, but thought better of it. I'm sure when it's finished, they will sort it out and make access and egress much easier. Silly me: making assumptions again. I thought it might already be that way.

The *coup de grace* was yet to come. I decided that we should visit Mirdiff, because I'm that kind of impulsive guy; always living on the edge, and we headed out of Vegetable City and along the Rashidiya road. About two kilos along it we spotted a brand new entrance to Festival City. How we laughed. If we'd stayed on this road to begin with, we'd have got there without having to drive an extra ten kilometres. Ah well, we know for next time.

As for Mirdiff, well, it's a weird place, right under the flight path towards Dubai International Airport. I went to look at a few villas there when I first came out, but the sound of low-flying passenger jets every two or three minutes put paid to that idea. I haven't been back since, the family hadn't seen it, and I wanted to try a burger at the new Gourmet Burger Kitchen branch, so that's where we went.

The GBK is in the Uptown development, which is a very European-style residential and retail development with large circular plazas and steep-roofed low-rise buildings containing shops and apartments. Last time I came to the development on a villa hunting trip only the Spinneys supermarket was open. This time the whole place was open, with lots of clothes shops and cafés to browse in or sit down for a drink in.

We found the GBK and ordered some burgers, chips and lovely-sounding chocolate-bar-themed milk shakes. We were the only customers in there initially, but soon other people started filtering in. One woman came in and asked if they did anything other than burgers, which Teresa found highly amusing, given the name of the place. The burgers arrived, rising like SZR towers from the plate, with thick patties, masses of salad and relish, all contained in a large sesame bun and held together with a large cocktail stick. They weren't edible in the traditional hand-held fashion and had to be dismantled before shoving gob-wards. I removed the lettuce and tomato and anything else slightly organic-looking and tucked in. Can you tell how the health kick is going?

The burgers were OK. Nice, but not the best burger I've ever had, I must say. The shakes were really good, though.

Tomorrow I could well end up in Doha again. They need me there, and I could be there a while this time. I don't mind, as long as I'm back for the arrival of my parents and brother.

Saturday, March 31, 2007
Arabian (Karaoke) Nights

More "Only in Dubai" moments over this last week, including the moment I walked into a bank and saw a man stood at the service desk with a brilliant-white specimen of a parakeet on his shoulder. I did a cartoon-style double-take and rubbed my eyes, but they were not deceiving me. I didn't bother to ask the man what was going on. I feared the bird might answer for him.

So, the Dubai World Cup is tonight, this being the Richest Horse Race In The World, of course. It runs in about ten minutes' time. If I was a betting man I would have to break the law in this country because under shariah law it is forbidden. The Maktoum family are mad on horses, especially Sheik Mohammad. He's not a horse; he's the ruler of Dubai, of course. He went to university in Cambridge and fell in love with horse-racing there, so the story goes, and now he owns the world-renowned Godolphin stables in Newmarket.

Of course, everyone knows that gambling *does* take place. It happens over phones and the internet. I've even heard whispered tales of bookies being flown in especially for the meeting, although I doubt they bring all their usual racetrack gubbins with them, such as the little stands and whiteboards to display prices on. These tales weren't literally whispered as such, but they were still told with a wry smile and a cynical tone. Things happen that shouldn't. It's the way of our crazy world...man.

As it is, this kind of event doesn't really interest me. It's more of a fashion show for shallow people who want to be seen in the right place, doing and saying the right things and getting completely shit-faced at the same time. Of course, I would say that because I didn't get invited on a corporate, otherwise I would have been there in a flash, pressing the flesh and guzzling the free bubbly. I'm a man of principle, after all.

I quite like to watch the gee-gees as it happens, even if I'm just a self-conscious, quid-each-way kind of gambler. I used to go to the races in Thirsk on occasion. It always made for a good family day out if the weather was good, and was unbelievably cheap: three quid to get in to the Family Ring, if I remember right. It's just a shame that the race meetings invariably turned Thirsk market place into a no-go area for anyone who was still sober after 7pm.

This bewilderingly reminds me of the other thing that links Dubai and Thirsk: Paul Scholes, of Manchester United, and formerly Engerlund. He was at Thirsk races the other year, and I also saw him the other week coming out of a hotel in Dubai on the day Man United beat Boro in the cup replay. It is, as they say, a small world, especially when you meet short, ginger-haired footballers twice in two completely different locales within two years. This probably has some cosmic meaning, and a connection with wormholes and super-string theory and all that, or I could just be talking bollocks again. I'll stick to cats in boxes.

Bollocks. I said that a lot last night. Our neighbours out the back decided to have a karaoke party last night, which is fine by me. I like a bit of karaoke now and again, especially as I can hold a tune quite well (even if I say so myself) and it always surprises people when I elbow them out of the way to prove this. The problem with last night was how they insisted on leaving the doors and windows wide open so that everyone within a hundred metres could hear their increasingly-croaky warbling and clapping and whooping as another twiddling *oud* kicked off another bloody song.

I might not have been so bothered if I'd known the tunes, but they were all completely unheard of where I hail from, and all of them sounded exactly the same to me. It was really quite annoying, because it was a cooler night and we wanted to have our window open, but that was impossible. The mechanical, brain-burrowing hum of the air-conditioning was what we resorted to in the end, as we shut the door in disgust. We could still hear the karaoke, however. The inevitable excitable crescendo of every song managed to over-power the glazing and the AC, and I lay there wishing for a Bon Jovi track in the first time in living memory. I was literally living on a prayer.

Eventually they shut the doors. This was at about 1.30am. I thanked my lucky stars and opened the window to let the cool night air in. Twenty minutes passed, and, just as sleep threatened to swallow me into its blissful inky depths, the doors opened again, and the warbling and clapping and croaky whooping crashed into my mind like a gang of Doc Marten-wearing orang-utans carrying buckets of custard and trampling all over a five-star gourmet buffet I was about to help myself from.

BOLLOCKS!

It went on for another thirty minutes, and by the time they finally shut the doors again, I had thought of every possible solution, most of which would have probably ended in me being arrested or at least beaten to a bloody pulp with karaoke microphones. I could have pleaded or just shouted off my bedroom balcony at them, but would that have helped? I don't know.

I know what kind of impolite and possibly violent response I'd get in the UK, but have no idea here, and being a guest of sorts here, I am reluctant to offend people, even if they're annoying me. Either that or I'm a coward, which explains why I'm venting here. I'm glad I wasn't pushed to the point where I would have found out their reaction for sure.

We had our revenge when we had a barbecue today. Martin and his boy came round and the kids made a load of noise in the garden while Teresa subjected our neighbours to the delights of ABBA's greatest hits. That'll learn 'em.

I wonder which nag won the race.

APRIL

Saturday, April 14, 2007

It'll be nice when it's finished.

I've been away for a while; not actually away from Dubai, but away from the computer. We've had visitors in town. My mum, dad and younger brother, Simon, left last night after a whirlwind week in this crazy (pronounced *kerr-ay-zee*) town. Their visit was a real eye-opener for them, and it has proved to be one for me as well.

It seems like a dream now, but just over a week ago, I picked the visitors up from the airport. Joseph and I were there, eagerly watching for their familiar faces to emerge from the swarm of humans passing through the automatic doors. I was nervous as hell, for some reason. My guts were in knots, and I'd had a really bad irritable bowel attack the previous night. Too much info, I guess, but I had barely slept either, even though I'd spent most of the day cleaning the house to what I thought would be an acceptable standard for my mother.

When I spied my brother's face emerging through the throng at the airport, the nervousness peaked, but after the greeting hugs and kisses, the butterflies were gone. My visitors looked absolutely shattered after their overnight flight and none of them had slept. They brightened up as we headed off through the light Friday morning traffic, and Joseph and I gave them a short guided tour of the main sights visible from the Sheik Zayed Road.

From then on it's all a blur really. I took another week of leave from work and we had a lot to cram in to a few days, so we did the obligatory brunch at the Marriott (on Easter Sunday), a day at the beach, a look at the malls, the Big Bus Tour, a visit to the fake designer Mecca otherwise known as Karama (where we were offered a "genuine fake Rolex" by an Indian chap on the street), a meal on Bateaux Dubai and finally a desert safari, which was the best-enjoyed event of the week, I believe.

Our visitors and I went on the safari - Teresa and the kids stayed behind this time - with a company called Desert Rangers, and, in all honesty, the experience was much better than with the previous tour company. Our driver, George, was a slightly mad chap from Goa who liked to sing along to '70s and '80s music whilst paying more attention to the two young ladies who joined our party in Arabian Ranches than to the road he was driving along.

His whole demeanour changed when we hit the dunes. He donned an old, moth-eaten, animal-skin hat and took great pleasure in showing us his excellent dune-bashing skills as he sped over the sand and twisted and turned his Land Cruiser this way and that, all with just one hand on the steering wheel.

I'm not sure if it was less scary this time or if I was just more prepared for it, but I wasn't half as frightened as I was last time. I think sitting in the middle row is the best option. My poor old Dad sat in the front seat next to George most of the time, and after we'd finished the most intense dune-bashing and had stropped right out in the desert near some camels, he almost fell out of the car looking whiter than a pint of milk with a cartoon poorly face drawn on it.

The Bedouin camp part at the end was really good as well. They fed us before the belly dancer arrived, and gave us ample opportunity to sample henna painting, shisha and drinks from the bar, as well as the chance to go on a short camel ride if we so wished. The food was generous and pretty good quality, and there was just a better vibe all round. More people danced with the belly dancer, and they completed the night with a few disco and dance classics to get us all gyrating on the carpet under the dark desert sky. I got another henna tattoo – a scorpion this time – but my mum patted me on the arm while we were queuing for food and the scorpion ended up looking like a disembowelled ladybird. I only cried a bit...to make her feel guilty, of course.

The only slight let-down was that we didn't see the sunset. As we drove through the desert, clouds moved across the sky and hid the sinking sun. This pattern of weather repeated itself most nights of the week, and my mum was slightly disappointed to leave Dubai having never seen a nice sunset over the sea or in the desert.

Also worth a mention is the Bateaux Dubai. As is customary, I got slightly wound up about getting there on time, since this restaurant is one that moves. When I made the booking I was told in no uncertain terms to get there by 8pm or we wouldn't get on, so when our taxi driver turned up at 7.20 with a long drive through Sharjah-bound traffic ahead, my heart sank. I asked him to get us there by 8pm, and he told me, "No Problem, Boss".

He weaved in and out of the traffic and sniffed out the least congested routes like some moustache-wearing bloodhound, and we got there right on schedule. I gave him a generous tip for his efforts and we trotted over to the glass-sided boat, walking towards the gangplank between two large, lighted crescents where we were greeted by smiling staff in crisp uniforms.

When we sat down, we noticed that the boat was half-empty, and we sat there until nearly 8.45pm waiting for everyone to turn up. We were ever so slightly peeved at this, and I couldn't believe I'd got so stressed about getting there on time. Personally, I hate tardiness. It reeks of disrespect and arrogance, and because these people couldn't get there on time, the journey was at least half an hour shorter than it should have been. The organiser's promise to leave bang on time was obviously an empty one; they wouldn't want to lose the revenue. As it was, the cruise ended just as we finished our coffees and paid our bills. We didn't get the chance to sit on the rear upper deck and sip an after-dinner drink whilst taking in the delights of the creek at night.

Despite this, the Bateaux experience and the meal were pretty damn enjoyable. We still had a good view of the creek from inside the boat, courtesy of the glass exterior. The creek takes on a completely different vibe at night; all the old mosques and souk buildings are lit up and dhows covered in hundreds of coloured lights glided silently past us, casting shimmering reflections on the water. I would definitely recommend it – as long as it leaves on time.

And now my parents and Simon have gone; their physical, tangible forms vanished from our lives again, and it's as if they were never here. It all happened so, so quickly and now I'm left feeling a bit flat and empty. Now I have to re-focus on work and our future in Dubai having looked forward to my family's visit for so long. I can also look forward to going home in the summer. It's only three months away now, and it should go quickly if we keep busy.

I mentioned the eye-opening aspects of my family coming here. I think one big realisation that has dawned on me over this last week is that Dubai is an absolutely great place to visit for a week or two on holiday. It has a lot to offer tourists. The Burj Al Arab, the Madinat and the desert safaris are stylish and exotic. My visitors enjoyed their time, there's no doubt about it, even if their favourite phrase was: "It'll be nice when it's finished!"

Those of us who live and work here on a long-term basis see the other, less attractive aspects of the place, and after that initial honeymoon period when you are blind to, or just ignore, the cracks in the walls and the dirt under the surface, it can start to grind away at your soul. Those of us who are here to work are doing so on nothing more than a temporary basis. We are guests who've been invited to build this new, shiny metropolis of the Middle East for the affluent of the world. What do we get out of it? We get a tax-free salary, an expat lifestyle and year-round sunshine. Well, whoop-e-doo.

The salary may well be officially tax free, but with all the municipality fees, school fees, service charges and registration fees added to the high rents and all the other bits and bobs they fail to mention when you are being enticed into moving here, you might as well be paying forty percent income tax.

The expat lifestyle? Well, for a family like ours, that's sitting on a beach, going to the mall and eating out every weekend. Wow, so enriching, isn't it? And that's if you're in the highest-earning five percent of expats. I could be being unfair on the place, but so far I have struggled to see anything more culturally substantial here. What culture there is here is either "borrowed" from other places or tucked away in a dusty corner. What they also don't advertise is the traffic and then danger on the roads, the constant dust, the noise and the utter shallow phoniness of the place.

Sunshine? I'll give them that, it is pleasant for five or six months of the year. The rest of the time you're stuck indoors because of the heat, so your life becomes a dash between the air-conditioned sanctuaries of home, car, office, shopping mall and hotel.

Oh, a good moan gets the juices flowing. It gets it all out of your system and off your chest. I've been told that life is what you make it, and I agree to an extent. Life is what you make it, if you have the means. If life is purely just what you make it, why do most people yearn for something else, why do people move to other countries? Why don't we just make the most of where we live and who we live with? It's what a good friend of mine has been telling me for years now when I decide to travel to yet another country: The Grass is Always Greener on the Other Side.

I've also been told that happiness lies within, and I'm starting to think that this is true. It helps to have good people around you; close friends and family, and recent events have brought that into very sharp focus. Do we have to learn to be happy with what we have, and not get obsessed with what others have and we don't? Should we just accept our lot and play the hand we are dealt, whether it's a silver spoon, a plastic fork or a wooden spear?

Idealistic dreams of everyone living equally are just that: dreams. It would be nice, but it ain't gonna happen. We all know so little about the world other than from own perspective, with our own two eyes. Understanding that there are other perspectives is half the battle of life, I reckon. It might make us all happier.

I have a lot of thinking to do. And the soapbox needs a rest.

Thursday, April 26, 2007
Down and Out in Doha

Not really; stranded, lonely and confused maybe, but what's new?

I'm stuck in Qatar for a few days. I have been here since last Saturday, waiting to get my Qatar residence visa. My company want me to have one for Qatar as well, for administrative reasons that I can't be arsed to go into. Let's just say it's more for their benefit that it is for mine, and helps with their company registration process or something. They are still thinking about whether I should stay in Dubai or move to Doha full time, but this had no bearing on it.

I'm not sure how long I'm going to be here, either. I've had the requisite blood test and chest X-ray done after the now-familiar queuing at various windows and waiting my turn. Thankfully, I had a friend with me this time, a Mister Fix-it if you like; a chap who works for our company who speaks Arabic and who can pull strings. It's the same guy who drives the complete wreck of a car that I had a ride in on my first visit here: Jamal from Sudan. Surprisingly, that car of his car is still going.

Jamal managed to get me through the blood test part quite quickly, but I ended up having to wait over an hour for an X-ray. The wait was made worse by the number of people who jumped the queue, most of them wearing dish-dashes, it must be said. They don't even need a Mister Fixit. I was seething at the injustice of it all, conveniently forgetting that I'd jumped past a queue of at least fifty people to get the blood test. All in all, however, the system seemed a bit more efficient than in Dubai. Or maybe I'm just imagining it having gone through it once already.

So now I have to wait for the results, and then I'll have to go to some other government building to have another blood test (finger prick) to establish blood group, and then go to have my fingerprints scanned. They used to take your fingerprints with Indian ink until recently, which meant you were left with black fingertips for about a week, but now they've caught up with the 21st Century and use electronic scanners. After that, I should get the visa a day or two later. You know what comes now: *Insha'allah!*

Luckily, I've been quite busy and the time has gone fairly quickly. We've had a lot of meetings about the Big Hole in the Ground, and I've been going here, there and everywhere to get different things sorted. I also went to the Traffic Department to get myself a temporary driving licence so I can use a hire car. This involved more queuing, a very quick eye test, (entire process: Ah! I see one of your eyes is very bad! Oh well! APPROVED) and a few short, barked conversations between Mr. Fix-it and veiled women at counters, but after only an hour I left with a credit-card-sized licence very similar to the UAE one, which will become a permanent licence when I get my visa.

So I now have the pleasure of driving around Doha, albeit in a car that has less power than a three-legged zebra wearing stilettos. It is different to Dubai because there is no Sheik Zayed Road-style twenty-lane highway going through it (although one is under construction). The main roads seem to be the six lane ring roads, all identified by a letter, such as C-ring road, etc., and there are traffic lights and roundabouts galore, which seems to put paid to any real speed. The roundabouts are a challenge; it's a bit of a free-for-all with people pulling out when they shouldn't and changing lanes without any warning. Traffic can build up at certain times in certain places, but generally moves at a better rate than in Dubai.

The worst part of the days has been the nights, if that makes sense. Going back to an empty hotel room is a pretty lonely experience. It's when I miss the family the most, and this time I seem to be missing them more. I think it's because Emma was upset when I got out of the car at the airport on Saturday. It's the first time she's done this kind of thing when I've left, and it broke my heart to see her crying because I was going away. Teresa tells me she has been asking for me, and Joseph keeps asking when I'm coming home. Unfortunately it looks like they're going to have to get used to me being away.

I'm in a different hotel this time because the Marriott was deemed too expensive, so I've ended up in the Movenpick Towers hotel at the West Bay end of the Corniche. It's almost brand new, having opened only four months ago. It smells new, with the smells of still-damp plaster and paint assaulting your nostrils as you walk around. The roads around it aren't even finished.

I think it's still going through teething problems. The hotel staff are over-the-top in their attentiveness to the point of being annoying, and the main restaurant serves lukewarm buffet food for breakfast, lunch and dinner. Most shockingly of all, for an international chain hotel, there is NO ALCOHOL.

I discovered this when the Russian concierge showed me round my pleasant-enough, dark wood furnished room. He opened the mini-bar fridge, and saw my eyes light up, and then told me the hotel is dry. After letting me cry on his shoulder for ten minutes or so, he told me soothingly that I could get my fix over the road at the Four Seasons Hotel. What have I said previously about consistency? This is a high-end, franchised hotel, so what is with the booze ban?

I followed the concierge's advice and went across the road; rather that than drink another fruit cocktail or watch a clumsy, nervous waiter taking a napkin-swaddled plastic bottle of water out of a champagne bucket. Ooh, it must be a vintage year for Evian.

On another night I thought I would try the noodle house restaurant in the hotel, and it was actually pretty good. The only thing that spoiled it was the presence of a plump American woman with a loud, whiny voice who was patronising her male work colleague. She was sat at a fair distance away from me - a distance you would assume would render normal conversation levels inaudible, or at least reduce it to a low murmur when combined with the oriental background muzak - but no, I heard every damned word of what she was saying. I was willing the waiter to bring some food and stuff it into her mouth.

As is customary on these occasions, I sat in the darkest corner available, reading a book and sipping a very nice glass of ginger ale while I waited for my food. Dining alone while working away from home is never the most enriching experience, particularly if you start talking to yourself out of loneliness. Other diners and restaurant staff tend to shoot you worried looks and are reluctant to start conversations. They can sense the desperation when you start talking at length about the weather.

An explanation is due now: I mentioned that the kids would have to get used to my absence. Unfortunately, they are going to have to get used to seeing me only every three or four months. Teresa and kids are going back to the UK. One reason is that they miss family and friends in the UK, and the recent visitors only brought these feelings into even sharper focus. On top of this, our principal aim of making some money over here just isn't working because Dubai is just too expensive, and Doha isn't much better. Villas are even more expensive here, and with the prospect of Emma starting school (on top of the ever-rising school fees), it has been decided that I will stay in the Middle East, work in Doha, and try to live as cheaply as possible. I'll probably be working for a different company, if things keep going as they are. I will go home twice a year, and the family will visit me once a year or so.

It isn't ideal, but it's the best option out of the few available, I believe. I could go home to the UK, but would face the prospect of a rather hefty tax bill having not spent a full tax year (April to April) out of the country. It's a stupid rule, if you ask me. I don't want to stay in Dubai alone. Well at all, really: I am starting to think that I've had my fill of the place.

Now I've got my first weekend in Doha ahead, and I have no idea what I'm going to do. At least I have a car to use now. Come on Qatar: Entertain me!

Saturday, April 26, 2008

Things To Do In Doha When You're Desperate (AGAIN!)

[The eagle-eyed amongst you will notice a bit of a jump forwards in time. This entry is from the blog about my short stint in Doha in Spring 2008. I've added it in because it is about a football match, and in light of the absolutely incredible decision to award the 2022 FIFA World Cup to Qatar, I'd thought it would be of interest.]

That was a quick weekend. An eventful one, mind you; but still quick, owing to the fact that it consisted of only one day: Friday.

In the morning I did a spot of shopping at the huge Carrefour in Villagio Mall. After dropping my shopping back at the flat, I sat around for a bit and decided I should get out and about while I still could, bearing in mind the approach of summer. I drove down to the Corniche, parked up just near the Emir's vast, palatial palace (funny that) and had a little wander on the path running along the bay. The Corniche has to be Doha's best feature, with grass and trees and an ever-changing view as you move along. Little dhows run cruises around the bay from jetties dotted along the length of it, and it is really quite a popular destination for residents, especially towards late afternoon and early evening when the temperature drops. Many just walk along it, taking in the air; kids frolic on the grass; some maniacs even jog. It's very pleasant.

Hunger seduced me away from the Corniche and I ended up at Fuddruckers, an American burger restaurant, but not a fast food joint by any means. Their burgers are pretty good, and you have the choice of a large range of toppings and sauces, which you help yourself to from a salad bar. I opted for a half-pound plain burger, which was more than ample. I couldn't even finish the fries that came with it, and I'm glad I didn't let greed get the better of me. I could have chosen the pound burger. A pound! That's a big packet of minced beef that you would use to feed a family of four with. It must be huge.

With my belly full, I left Fuddruckers and sauntered back to the car, wondering how I'd spend the rest of my evening. It was only early; about 5.30pm, and I didn't really want to go to a bar. I wouldn't be able to drink unless I got a taxi, and with only one day off for the weekend, it's a bit of a chew. As it was, I spotted the bright floodlights of the nearby stadium, just past the tennis complex, and wondered if a football game was on. I drove closer to it as I made my way onto the main road and saw the large electronic scoreboard lit up with two club crests and the score-line of 0-0. It might have already kicked off, but chances were that it was only early in the game, so I drove round to the stadium itself. There were a few cars there, but it wasn't packed by any means, so I parked close to a set of stairs leading up to the stands and ambled up them. A man was selling tickets at the first landing, and he told me it was the princely sum of ten riyals. I asked who was playing and he smiled at me as if I was a simpleton and should automatically know, and didn't actually answer. Still, I decided it would be worth a watch. I like to see football games in different countries, as much to sample the different atmospheres as anything. It was good decision.

From the enormous electronic scoreboard and the flags hoisted all around I was able to establish that the match was between Qatar Sporting Club and Al Khor, and there was a crowd of about fifteen hundred or so in a stadium that could hold maybe ten thousand. Many of the people watching were local men, dressed in their familiar, brilliant white dish-dashes, made even more squint-inducing by the floodlights. Some had football scarves on, some carried drums of different shapes and sizes. There wasn't a single woman that I could see in the ground apart from one Western woman who walked past with her partner as I entered. Seating was a help-yourself, first-come-first-served affair, and I parked myself near the top row, just about level with the penalty area. I soon realised that this was a big game by how professional everything looked. There were cameras everywhere and electronic advertising boards lined every side of the luscious, green pitch. They even had one of those little electric buggies to carry injured players off the pitch. It was driven in the style of a white Land Cruiser, presumably.

When the game kicked off at 6.30 or so, with Qatar SC in yellow and Al Khor in blue, the drumming and chanting started, all conducted by a large man in a yellow T-shirt who stood on the front row with his back to the action. I couldn't help but smile. The throbbing rhythms and enthusiastic chanting won me over straight away. The noise ebbed and flowed with the game, which was played at a good pace considering the climate. Within two minutes there was a goal for the home side as a hapless defender glanced a long, raking cross past his 'keeper. The drums and chants became louder and confetti fluttered down from the stands. Then, after another minute, Al Khor had equalised after a free-kick from the left edge of the penalty area was smashed into the opposite corner. I laughed and shook my head. Utter madness.

Sadly, the action died down a bit, but there were still moments of excitement. Some of the attacking play was quite impressive, but then some of the defending was of the slapstick variety. I couldn't see it finishing 1-1. Qatar Sports Club's defence looked particularly shaky, especially with a very short goalkeeper who was good at shouting, but not so good at coming for high balls. The first half ended with Qatar SC earning a penalty and taking the lead.

Half time's arrival means only one thing wherever you watch a game: refreshment. I'd seen people coming down the steps with packets of pumpkin seeds, *shwarmas* and little cartons of juice or water. I left my seat to find the source of the food and drink and saw a man at the top of the stand with boxes of the stuff I wanted, so I bought a drink and a packet of seeds for the princely sum of two riyals, and returned to my seat for the second half.

The second period was a story of missed chances. Al Khor pressed for an equaliser and Qatar played on the break, splitting the defence time and again, but missing every time. The local supporters became more and more frustrated, shouting, "YALLAH!" whenever they broke, then tutting and stamping frustrated sandals onto the concrete when they again failed to score. The odd English term could be heard, such as "shoot" or "offside", but sadly I never heard an, "Abdullah, you're shite!" I don't know what the Arabic is for that.

As it was the home team held on for the win, as far as I know. I left the game with a minute or two of injury time to go, mainly to beat the rush. As I left, a local teenager held his scarf over his head and grinned at me. "Winners!" he said as I passed him. I smiled and nodded. This is what makes the game of football what it is. Cultural divides just melt away when it comes to willing your team to stick the ball in the onion bag. Or it could be goatskin sack.

Later on I had a look on the net about Qatar Sporting Club, and found out that they have some big names, or at least formerly big names, on their books, like Christophe Dugarry, Claudio Cannigia and Marcel Desailly. I don't think any of the big names played last night, but one could be wrong. The number 23 looked kind of familiar. The announcements were all in Arabic, naturally, so the names could have been mispronounced or lost in the indecipherable-to-my-ears language. The one name I remember hearing was Karkouri, who used to play for Charlton Athletic in England. It also transpires that the match I saw the was Emir's Cup quarter-final, and QSC are now in the semi-final, to be played on 3rd May.

[And back to 2007 we go!]

Saturday, April 28, 2007

Weekends - Doha style.

I have just spent my first weekend in Doha. The potential for loneliness and boredom was high, so what better way to waste the hours than drive around the place exploring and getting one's bearings? And with the loneliness and boredom at the forefront of my worries, I combined my exploration on Friday with looking for a PSP games console. I decided that now I am going to be alone for long spells, I need something to alleviate the boredom. So out I went.

Dubai has a lot of shopping malls. It's supposedly one of the attractions of the place. On a stupidly hot day, what is better than wandering around an air-conditioned temple of consumerism or sitting in Starbucks sipping on a half-fat soy latte?

And what Dubai can do, Doha wants to do better.

There are a surprising amount of malls here. The main, most popular one is the Doha City Centre Mall (they seem to have City Centre Malls in all the major cities in the Gulf). It has an ice rink, a cinema and lots of shops, including the ubiquitous Carrefour. It also has lots of shops that are not yet open and new extensions with massive hotels being constructed all around it.

As I said, I was looking for a PSP, so I tried in Carrefour. They only had pink ones, and I am not having a pink one. Call me traditional and gender-role-compliant, but pink just isn't my colour; I insist on my Barbie dolls wearing blue. I also tried a few other shops in the mall. No luck there either. They seem to be in short supply, unless you're a girl, so it was time to explore Doha.

It is very quiet on a Friday; the roads are almost empty, a lot of the shops are just closed, or don't open until after lunch. It reminded me of how Sunday used to be in the UK many years ago. As it was, I didn't actually head out until the afternoon, so the malls were at least open, if not all the shops within them. Some closed for Friday prayers, others didn't. It is mostly pot luck as to which ones you can find open, unless you can fathom out what their patterns are.

Looking on the map I had borrowed from the hotel I spotted the Sports City area and a new mall called Villagio nearby, which sounded promising. I pointed the car out towards the desert, and drove along a quiet, straight boulevard lined with closely-grouped, crane-like lampposts that were each adorned with little halogen spotlights. Within a short time I saw the elongated egg-cup shape of the Aspire tower and the skeletal roof of the Khhlifa stadium, which they used for the Asian Games last autumn. Impressive structures they are. I drove round the empty car-park for a bit, allowing myself different views of the buildings.

I find there is something eerily peaceful about sports venues when they are empty. They stand like this for the greater part of their existence; sleeping in dignified, empty silence and waiting to wake up to the noise and colour of a sports event to bring everything to life again as the car parks fill up, the crowds take their seats, the concession operators and programme sellers fill the concourses, and the competitors take to the field in pursuit of glory and adulation...or booing, if it's Boro's Riverside Stadium.

Right next door to the stadium is the new Villagio shopping mall. In contrast to the sports stadium, this place is awake a lot more than it is asleep (except on Friday mornings, of course). After I'd finished looking at the stadium, I drove into the car park of the mall and parked as near to the mall as I could. As I approached, I couldn't help but notice the intended theme of the mall. Even the exterior is built to resemble an Italian town, giving the effect of pastel-coloured buildings of different shapes and sizes huddled together. Even so, I didn't expect to see what I found inside.

As I entered the mall, I was immediately aware of the similarities with Ibn Battuta mall in Dubai, where the malls boulevards and shops are styled and themed to make you feel like you are in an old Andalusian village or ancient China. Villagio is themed on Venice, and the premise of closely-huddled, terracotta-roofed buildings is even more prevalent inside. The ceiling of the mall is painted to look like a summer sky; azure blue with wispy clouds here and there. The floor is tiled to resemble a Venetian street, and there are ornate lampposts dotted along the walkways.

It's when you look down from the fake sky that you notice it: right in the middle of this mall is a canal. There are even real, life-sized gondolas that you can actually ride in. Not for the first time, the word Vegas sprung into my head, as I shook it side to side in disbelief. One of these days my head is going to fall off with all the shaking it does.

So I started walking along the canal in the fake Venice. I stopped briefly to look up when I heard a bird singing from the roof of one of the shops. I couldn't see a bird, but it sounded real enough. I wouldn't have been surprised if it had been coming from a loudspeaker. Walking further along, I crossed the canal over an ornate bridge, and turned a corner to find a food court and a large area surrounded by high white hoardings that was obviously not finished. Who knows what lies there? I've been told since that it may be an ice rink. It's not quite Ski Dubai standard, I'm sure, but the ambition is there, you just know it.

As it happens, the Villagio visit didn't produce what I was looking for. The huge Carrefour (is there any other size?) again offered only pink PSPs. I was told to try the Virgin Megastore by a shop assistant, and did so, but while they had loads and loads of games and accessories for PSPs, they didn't have a single PSP. How annoying.

I wearily headed back towards the car park, stopping for a late lunch of lentil soup and bread at a French-style cafe. There were no Italian cafes, which struck me as peculiar in a replica Venice. Maybe they were still building them.

As I drove away from Villagio - having to drive further along the main road in order to double back at the next lights - I noticed yet another mall, just past it; right next to it, in fact. It was a much older one, and was called the Hyatt Plaza or something like that. At the front, near the road, there was a giant - I hesitate to call it a sculpture - model of a shopping trolley. It must have been thirty or forty metres high, at a guess. So it's not just Dubai that has a taste for the incredibly kitsch and mind-boggling. This kind of thing belongs in a U2 concert, or a pulp sci-fi novel about giant killer shopping trolleys.

As I approached the actual mall, its age showed. It was in need of some love and attention, or at least a fresh coat of paint. There was a large hypermarket with a name I can't remember, and a cluster of small shops, fast-food outlets and kiddies play areas all around it. I tried the big shop for a PSP, but was again frustrated. Not even close. This particular hypermarket was really low-end, I thought. It made Netto look classy.

Frustrated by my lack of success in getting my sweaty mitts on a PSP, I thought about other options. The hotel has a swimming pool, and a bit of exercise would do no harm. I could even have a Jacuzzi without turning the bubbles on after the kinds of food I'd eaten. So I looked for swimming shorts. I found some, and every single pair was size L. The dead-eyed shop assistant I collared looked me up and down and shrugged, mumbling something about the size L being generous. He pointed me towards a changing room, inviting me to see for myself.

I say changing room; it was actually four planks of MDF held together with nails and plonked in the middle of the clothing section as an afterthought. The "door" didn't have a lock; it had a shoe-lace and a metal eyelet to tie it around. It did have a mirror, I'll give them that. So I squeezed into this little structure and tried on the shorts, being careful not to bump the walls of the structure for fear of knocking it down, leaving me standing there in the middle of a low-rent hypermarket with my trousers round my ankles.

As luck would have it, the swimming shorts were of a generous size, and they fit me, so I made my purchase and left the shop. On my way out, I spied a small electronics shop that I had missed earlier to one side, and through the window I saw a range of PSPs in a range of manly colours. *GET IN YA BEAUTY!*

As usual, salvation came from an unexpected source. I dived into the shop, bought a PSP and made my way back to the hotel with my newest toy in a bag and the smile of a ten-year-old boy on my face.

I also bought a couple of games: Pro Evolution Soccer and Call of Duty. I was somewhat worried when I noticed that they had the wrong region number on them for my new PSP, but after a quick battery charge, I inserted the little disc, the console had a little think about it, the software updated and all was well. The games are great, and look great. Pro Evo plays and looks almost exactly the same as it does on the PS2 / X-box. OK, the commentary isn't so good, and you can't edit the strips, but that's not an issue to me. I now have something to waste the lonely hours with.

Saturday came, and I decided to go for that swim in the hotel. The first part of this venture was to push down and swallow the fear of heights I have. The pool was on the twenty-sixth floor, which is high enough for me, thank you, even though I have lived on the twenty-ninth floor before, during a short working stint in the USA.

Luckily the pool was enclosed, not open-air, so I donned my new shorts and took the lift from my room on the seventh to the twenty-sixth floor. I was impressed with how fast the lift moved, and I watched the electronic display count them off at a floor every second or so. I had visions of it shooting out of the top of the building *a la* Willy Wonka's glass elevator, but it came to a quick stop at 26 and I stepped out into the lobby.

The views from up there were spectacular. The pool area was surrounded by full-height windows giving a superb view across the bay and along the sweeping arc of Corniche. As I stood there, I watched an airliner taking off from the distant Doha airport. It rose slowly and quietly towards me, before passing over and to the side of the building and heading out towards the Persian Gulf. At a hundred or so metres in the air, everything looks tiny on the ground. I can only imagine what the view will be like from the top of the building I am working on, which will be nearly a hundred floors and four hundred metres high. I might struggle to contain my vertigo for any length of time if I eventually go up it. Like with most fears I have, the key seems to be confronting them and reducing their impact by just getting on with it.

I had a little swim, then ordered some lunch to eat at a table right next to the window, looking out across the calm blue bay and down at the green arc of the Corniche. It was really quite pleasant and relaxing.

The afternoon was spent playing a few games on the PSP, completing a couple of tough missions in war-torn Europe before seeing off Newcastle 7-0. I think a combination of the two games would be entertaining. Hoying a few grenades at the Geordie midfield would certainly liven things up.

And then Saturday night was upon me. I ventured over to the Ramada Hotel on C-ring road and found an expat bar with big screens and a smoky, working men's club vibe. It was called *Shezadne* or something. After watching some English football for a while, I went for a very reasonable curry at the Bombay Balti in the newer part of the hotel. A very kind lady from the reception had guided me all the way there, telling me it was popular and always very busy. It wasn't. I was the only one there.

To round off the night, I went to the Library bar at the Four Seasons Hotel, just across the road from my hotel. The bar is a pleasant, quiet bar, with dark wood panels on the walls, large sofas to lounge in, and some delicious mini-poppadums to snack on. It has the feel of an old-fashioned gentlemen's club. It was quiet in the bar, and no-one was brave enough to strike up conversation with me, so I had a couple of whiskies and gingers (something I've just started drinking after I got the idea from my old man), a cigar (which is naughty, but I didn't inhale) and a read of the local English-language paper.

I returned to my hotel room and caught a movie just starting on TV, which was entertaining enough, and then I went to sleep. I'm loath to say I'm becoming used to this lifestyle, but it's getting easier to bear. It's not terribly exciting, and I'm missing Teresa and the kids, but I'm still not missing Dubai.

MAY

Monday, May 07, 2007

A Life of Goodbyes

I'm still in Doha. Strange forces are at work – or maybe they've taken a holiday – and I am still waiting for my residence permit to be granted. I thought it would only take a week, maybe two. My company said the same and are going to have a big hotel bill at this rate.

Staying in a hotel alone for over two weeks is not really my idea of fun, especially in a hotel that is completely disorganised and still finding its feet. The fact that the staff are in your face all the time, bowing and scraping and grinning like simpletons makes it even more annoying. I've taken to staring at the floor as I walk about just to avoid them. It doesn't work. I suppose they are only doing their job, but come on guys, stop laying it on so thick. If I want something from you, I will ask you.

At least the weekend was a bit more interesting. Once it was clear I wasn't going to get away last week, I booked Teresa and kids on a flight from Dubai on Thursday night and they arrived at around 5.30pm. I picked them up at the airport and then we all trundled back to the hotel. When they emerged from the arrivals area, I saw that Teresa was wearing a strappy top, with her shoulders bared. I advised her to cover up with a cardigan or scarf as soon as she could. Qatar isn't as liberal as Dubai in its attitudes. We're all still learning about the ways of this world. The family were pleased to see me, at least, and I was definitely pleased to see all of them, even after only two weeks away. As we drove along the Corniche, they took in the different surroundings and remarked on the lack of cranes and traffic. Five minutes into the journey, Joseph exclaimed: "this place is much better than Dubai!" Well, thought I, don't judge *this* book by its cover.

I took the liberty of booking an extra room for the kids, which meant I had to decamp to the twenty-first floor, so they could give us adjoining rooms with a door between them. Privacy for Mummy and Daddy was the order of the day. Joseph was impressed with having his own mini-bar and TV to watch, but most of all, he was excited at the prospect of swimming in the twenty-sixth floor swimming pool. Emma was excited at having a huge bed to sleep in. There might at last be some room for the extensive menagerie of soft toys that seems to follow her everywhere.

It was an early night that first night. After a quick bite in the restaurant we pretty much hit the sack straight away. Everyone was whacked, but I still found myself listening to the wind whistling around the corners of the building. With the curtains shut, it was hard to tell we were at a height, but when I remembered where I was, I had to swallow the rising terror back down before it became more than a nagging, but manageable fear. I know, I know; I'm a big scaredy-cat.

So Friday dawned, and we had a leisurely morning eating breakfast, watching telly, playing on the PSP and so on. Then we tried to go swimming, but found out that the pool was closed over the weekend for maintenance. Grrrrea: two disappointed children and not a clue what to do. The hotel, in its infinite wisdom, had no alternatives to offer me. It was too hot to go outside, so the zoo and the beach were out of the question.

In the end we drove to the Villagio mall to see something the kids have never seen before: a themed shopping mall. Well, OK, a themed shopping mall with a canal going through it. And they got to see the Asian Games stadium, the Aspire tower and the giant shopping trolley. This is the stuff dreams are made of, people. They will tell their grandchildren about this...when they want to make them go to sleep, possibly.

Anyway, on this particular visit to Villagio, I was with other people for the first time, so I discovered one of the unique features of the mall. Near the major entrance areas to the mall there are large two circular plazas with high, domed ceilings. One has a bright blue, day-time sky painted on it; the other a starry, night-time sky. But if you stand anywhere under the domed ceiling and talk, it echoes all around the plaza. You don't even to have to shout to get an echo. I didn't know this when I visited last weekend because the only voices were the ones in my head. But now I was with my noisy children. Of course, once this was discovered by Emma, she started whooping and screeching and giggling as the echoes of her voice bounced around the plaza.

Most of the shops and restaurants were closed as it was just approaching lunchtime, so we moved to the City Centre mall, which is nearer the hotel. I remembered that they had the ice rink there, and they also had ten-pin bowling, so there was at least some potential for something to do other than walk around malls. So after lunch we headed down to the optimistically-named Winter Wonderland (i.e. an ice rink), but there was nothing doing there either. You had to buy your own socks for the ice-skating, and the timings were all to pot, with sessions starting every few hours. As for the bowling alley, that was taken over by a birthday party.

What a fabulous weekend we were having. If I had been trying to sell Doha as a place to live for the family, I might have been more successful trying to persuade them to eat raw camel's testicles. We eventually returned to the hotel and the kids watched TV for a couple of hours before boredom got the better of me and I decided we would get out of the hotel and head to Rydges Plaza and have dinner at their better-than-average Italian restaurant. And that's what we did, before heading back and putting the kids to bed.

Saturday was much the same: a lazy day, without anything much to do. We whiled away the hours in the hotel and here and there, and before long it was time for Teresa and kids to go back to Doha airport and make their way home. I stayed with them for half an hour in the coffee shop until it was time to check in, then said goodbye. Again, it was Emma who made a fuss, and she cried and wailed as her buggy was pushed through the security scanners towards check-in. I waved one last time then returned to the car, alone again.

A refrain ran through my head all the way back along the Corniche towards the hotel: It sucks, it truly sucks. I hate saying goodbye, even though I have said it so many times in my life. My whole life seems to have been one goodbye after another, from my childhood when we moved every three years because of my father's work, to the teenage years at boarding school, to my adult life spent travelling to different places around the world for work and for life-enriching experiences. This is the price to pay: the life of goodbyes. It hurts now as much as it ever has, especially when I've got such a close bond with my wife and children. Worst of all, I know that I am going to have to separate myself from them for longer periods when they go back to the UK and I stay here, or go wherever I go. That is going to be really hard.

I have choices, of course, and I have to think it all over. Do I go back to the UK with them and face a massive tax bill? There's my health to worry about as well. When I am on my own, I have lower self-control. I get bored and lonely. My self-discipline weakens and I eat and drink to comfort myself. That could be a bad thing for me, with my high blood pressure, high cholesterol and high poundage, as well as an arrhythmia to contend with. My only hope is that I can throw myself fully into work and keep myself occupied and think of the money that I'm earning which will give my family a good life in the future.

I'm getting all maudlin again. Let's get back to Saturday night, after I dropped Teresa and kids off. That's when things got really, really weird.

I arrived back at the hotel to find it in near-darkness. The power was down. Rumours were rife: someone told me that there was a cable-strike in a nearby site, and the whole area was affected. Another hotel worker told me that the whole of Doha was without power. I looked through the windows, back along the Corniche and across at the Four Seasons Hotel, seeing all the lights that were quite obviously working and wondered as to the poor man's sanity. He had probably had several sweaty businessmen spraying spittle in his face already, so I spared him my particular brand of ashen-faced, menacingly monotonic complaint-making. In the lobby area people milled around like moths without a light to bounce off, members of staff bowed lower than ever before, and lights blinked and dimmed on and off. The lifts appeared to be working, but I didn't trust them at all.

I was slightly annoyed, as I had some work to do. The problem with being stranded in Doha is that I've struggled to keep in touch with some of the other jobs I work on back in Dubai. I've had several phone-calls from the boss, alternating between sympathetic, best-mate banter and blood-curdling ranting at my lack of omnipotence. So I ended up needing to do some work, and the power cut was surely the last straw: no access to computers or internet.

I spent an hour waiting for the power to return sitting in the hotel cafe drinking the complimentary soft drink I was offered, and then strode across the road to the Four Seasons, deciding enough was enough. They had also suffered a power cut, but they had a back-up generator that powered the entire hotel, and not just a few essential systems. It must be some bloody beast to do that job, thought I. The Four Seasons complex is huge. Luckily for me, the business centre was fully operational, and best of all, it was cheaper than the one in the Movenpick, so I was able to do the work I had to do, before treating myself to a snack and a couple of drinks in the Library bar. Because I'm worth it.

When I returned to my own hotel there were still no lights on in the windows of the guest floors. I approached the reception desk and asked a grey-suited, smiling man with big, brown, puppy-dog eyes for any new information. He deflected my queries with a straight bat and, having spotted my British English-tinged with-Yorkshire speech patterns, embarked on a bizarre and frankly unsettling critique of Great Britain.

Yes, the English language came from England; I am aware of that.

No, it's not a paradise; nowhere is.

No, it hasn't been the same since Lady Diana died… so very, very sad…

You *what?*

When he started with the Diana stuff I had to walk away before I poked him in the eye with the blunt end of an alcohol-free champagne bottle. I think I let an involuntary, "for fuck's sake," slip out as I turned away. Thinking about it now, it could well have been a ruse to get rid of me, and a clever one at that.

After more milling about and more shrugging platitudes but little in the way of hard facts from the hotel staff, I ended up sitting at a table on the outdoor terrace with a couple of Dutch chaps and a permanently grinning Malaysian guy till nearly 11.30pm. We talked about Dubai and Doha and anywhere else we could think of. We smoked Marlboro Lights and drank Sprite. We considered moving to a place that sold alcohol, but couldn't really be arsed. It was a pleasant distraction, even if one of the Dutch guys was sharcashtic beyond reason. The night became even more surreal when a green Jeep Wrangler came hurtling round the long bend in the road going past the hotel, rising onto two wheels in the style a stunt car in some blockbuster movie. It carried on moving on two wheels for a while before disappearing round the corner. If there hadn't been other people there to witness it, I might have thought I was hallucinating.

In the end, with no prospect of power returning soon, we all decided to risk the lifts and made our way to our darkened rooms, leaving the increasingly hysterical complainers in reception to their pointless ranting and the increasingly desperate hotel staff to their calming gesticulations. They were kind enough to provide us with torches to find our way round the dark corridors and at least the electronic locks on the room doors still functioned. Fortunately, the lack of air conditioning hadn't caused the hotel to heat up too much. It's just as well the power had gone off later in the day and not in the morning. The place would have been like a greenhouse.

I slept quite well, and was woken up at 5am when the lamp in the corner of the room suddenly came on and the air conditioning began to hum. I went back to sleep and woke up at 7am to an empty, quiet room. The whole power cut episode had done the job of distracting me from the previous evening's goodbyes. Distraction, it seems, is the key.

Sunday, May 13, 2007

Party on...

Summer is returning. The sun is getting hotter. The air is starting to feel thick with heat and moisture, and the vicious, unrelenting glare of the sun and its refection on every surface is getting brighter and brighter. The glass windows of buildings feel warm from the inside rather than cold and you notice the difference when you enter or exit a building. The air conditioning makes you shiver momentarily as you enter. On the other hand getting into a car - especially when it has been parked in the sunshine - is like entering a sauna but with a red hot steering wheel to hold.

My third weekend in Doha has been and gone and there is still no sign of the residence visa. I'm starting to think I'll never get it. On Thursday, I spent the day recoiling from a barrage of sardonic e-mails from a jumped-up little shit-bag in the client's Dubai office who seemed to have it in for me that day. I was glad of the opportunity to take a bit of a flier from work and drive down to the site on the Corniche to attend a little party they were holding to celebrate the end of a particular phase of work in the Big Hole in the Ground.

I got there just in time. The meeting room was full of people standing with their arms folded, looking longingly at the Arab-style feast laid out on the tables in the middle, with kebabs, pickles, hummus and flat-breads waiting to be consumed. Two large, oval plates took centre stage, but foil concealed the delights upon them. The Project Managers made their little speeches, the staff applauded politely, and then everyone eagerly tucked in.

The foil was ripped away from the two large plates to reveal the almost complete roasted carcasses of lambs (or possibly goats, it was hard to tell for sure) lying on beds of saffron rice. I waited a moment to see what would happen; half-expecting the lambs to get up and walk away, and then watched as the others around me dived in and started ripping the meat from the carcasses with their bare hands. They all used their right hands. No-one uses their left hand to touch food here, for reasons of hygiene. Left hands are for dealing with sanitary matters, shall we say.

So I dived in as well, feeling like some stone-age hominid without a spear or a loin cloth as I tore cooked flesh from the bones of the dead beast in front of me, piled it onto my plastic plate, and then stuffed it into my mouth. It felt good, and it tasted even better. I wouldn't like to hazard a guess as to when this animal had been gambolling around in a field, completely unaware of its final destiny in life, but I imagine it wasn't long ago.

This thought, along with the sight of the lamb's body with leg bones and ribs protruding from it might have put some people off, but there weren't many around me that showed any signs of being so. Within ten minutes, there wasn't much meat left at all; just bones and gristle and skin, as if a pack of ravenous hyenas had just taken its fill, before washing it all down with a can of Coke.

Greasy hands and faces were wiped clean and Arabic sweets were passed round. They were a kind I hadn't seen before; a sort of sticky, orange, crispy cigar filled with custardy cream. One was more than enough for me and then the party seemed to break up. Everyone began to shuffle away from the meeting room, wiping their mouths clean as they went back to their desks or made their way off site. A few of the big cheeses were meeting for a cup of tea in another room, but I decided against joining them - not that I'm a big cheese, more of a Dairylea triangle, if I'm honest - and slipped back to my car for the short drive back to my hotel.

With the sun dipping towards the horizon and the air cooling off, I decided to park up next to the Corniche and take in a little fresh air. I didn't walk very far, deciding to sit on the thick, white, concrete block wall at the water's edge and watch the world go by. Joggers, families and random single people passed by; now and again one of them greeted me with, "*Asala'am alaykum,*" as they passed. I still haven't got the hang of answering in Arabic automatically, favouring a nod or the quick, "Hi," in reply. I hope they aren't offended. No-one's punched me yet, anyway.

After fifteen minutes of peaceful reflection, I went back to the car and completed my journey to the hotel, wondering what I was going to do for the weekend, since it was upon me once more, and I was alone again. I ended up ringing a South African chap who works for one of the companies I deal with and we agreed to meet at the Australian bar in Rydges. We'd both had hard days, so a quick drink was definitely on the cards.

We met and chatted and drank, and I was introduced to a handful of people from various places and various companies - mostly construction related - and had a thoroughly pleasant evening drinking the black stuff and smoking other people's cigarettes. I know it's is a filthy habit, especially when you take one without asking. Oh well, they're only 90p a packet here, and if I bought my own I would smoke more, and I really shouldn't smoke, even on this ad-hoc, "only when I drink" basis. On top of alcohol it's just asking for trouble with this sensitive ticker of mine...I'm rattling on about my health again, aren't I?

The bar was pretty busy by 10pm. The music gradually got louder, and so did the people, and when I decided to leave at 11.30, there was a small group of people outside waiting to get in, standing impatiently on the other side of the velvet rope being guarded by gargantuan, glowering bouncers. I smiled to myself as I walked past them all and into the waiting lift. I've been there before, and I'm sure I'll be there again. Everyone wants to get in somewhere, and everyone wants to keep everyone else out. Unless you're a VIP, of course.

Friday was lie-in day. Though I miss my children, the one advantage of being away from them is not having them jumping all over me at 6.30 in the morning on a weekend. So I had a nice long sleep, before ordering room service for breakfast and watching old movies on the TV, sitting there in a hotel-issue bath robe that just about pulled together at the front.

Boredom got the better of me by early afternoon, so I decided to ring another chap, this time an ex-colleague from the Doha branch, who had suggested earlier last week that we visit the infamous Garvey's for a drink and some food. Their roast dinners are legendary, especially in their own lunchtime.

He picked me up and we drove out of central Doha, in the direction of the Sports City area, and eventually arrived at a complex tucked away from view behind some shops and villas. The complex is officially known as The European Families Club, and consists of a collection of single-storey buildings, including villas and fitted-out portacabins which they rent out to expats. Garvey's is the bar, and is accessed through a solid, dark wooden door next to the swimming pool area. Even on this stupidly hot day, the pool area was busy with lobster-skinned Brits sitting in the midday sun supping cold beers. Unfortunately, there were no canines with mental health issues anywhere to be seen.

Garvey's itself has been described as having the feel of a working men's club, and this assessment is difficult to argue with. It had obviously undergone a recent revamp, with fancy wooden Venetian blinds being added to the windows and dark blue paint slapped on the walls, but it can't betray its roots. The tables and chairs were old and wobbly and the once-white ceiling tiles now resembled a heavy smoker's teeth; yellowy-brown and quite unpleasant. Newer, cleaner tiles fitted with recessed lights had been fitted, obviously to provide some extra light, but they just served to highlight the griminess of their older neighbours. In the corner, a wall-mounted flat-screen TV showed sport on a permanent loop, interspersed with information about forthcoming Karaoke and Quiz nights and messages imploring people not to drink and drive. The obligatory pool table, dart board and large screen telly hid round a distant gloomy corner.

The clientele all seemed jolly enough when we entered: There was a mix of middle-aged, shaven-headed men in long shorts and replica football shirts, younger men in long shorts, football shirts and designer sunglasses, women in short skirts and cropped tops who were trying to ignore their young, boisterous children, and a few older, red-bonced men in long shorts and football shirts with faded tattoos extolling the virtues of female parents on every scrap of bare skin. A lot of these people were oil and gas workers and their families, I guessed, here to work on the tools on off-shore and on-shore installations.

My colleague informed me it was still early, and it was reasonably quiet for now, but most of these people would spend all day in this one place. Fights were quite a regular occurrence in the later hours, he told me.

Before I come across as some sort of insufferable snob (moi?), I must point out that the food in Garvey's is superb. I plumped for leek and potato soup and roast beef with all the trimmings, and was not disappointed. In fact, it wasn't just excellent, it was really cheap compared to the prices I've become used to paying in hotels in the region. The soup was as good as anything my mother could rustle up, the roast potatoes were crunchy without being greasy and the beef was just a little bit pink in the middle, and all covered in dark, thick gravy. Oh yes. The only slight let-down was the Yorkshire pudding, which was a little on the soggy side, but it didn't ruin the whole experience of eating a home-made roast dinner again.

When I'd eaten everything on my plate like a good boy (except the cauliflower, which I draw the line at), I sent my wife a cheeky text message telling her what I'd just eaten. Her reply was short, sweet and succinct: BOG OFF.

After a couple of non-alcoholic drinks (don't let the halo slip, now), my colleague and I headed off into the cooling late afternoon. It had certainly been an experience, that's for sure. It's like a real, authentic piece of UK culture has been lifted from a Northern industrial town and transplanted into the middle of this Middle Eastern city. The only hint that you're not in the UK is the high percentage of Asian staff behind the bar. It serves its primary purpose, which is to give people a home from home while they are overseas, and it keeps people happy...and drunk. Of course, I could get up on my soap-box and harp on about cultural assimilation and the criticism immigrants to the UK suffer because of their perceived lack of integration, but that would be remiss of me. It's been done to death, frankly.

Friday night was a lazy night. I watched Mission Impossible III on the hotel pay-per-view system, and it passed the time. When will that Tom Cruise fellow start showing his age? Lucky sod.

If Friday was a lazy night, Saturday was a lazy day. I spent it almost entirely in the hotel, only leaving it to get some lunch across the road in the neighbouring Four Seasons hotel, and having a little wander around the grounds to look at their impressive multi-level, lagoon-style swimming pool. The rest of the day I spent watching TV or playing the PSP, in between contemplating my future. I have two solid job offers for other work on the table now. One is in Doha, the other in Moscow, and I keep changing my mind as to which would be the better one to take. For one reason or another, I have pretty much decided to leave the company I'm with now. It's been on the cards for a while, quite honestly.

And here we are at the start of another week. I should finally get my visa and get home this week...home being Dubai, of course. It's strange how I see it like that now. But home is where the heart is, and my heart is with three people who I miss. I miss them a lot.

Saturday, May 19, 2007
Home is where the heart sort of flutters and jumps about

Finally back in Dubai.

Finally, I never thought I'd be so glad to be back here.

My last day in Doha consisted of waiting around a lot and witnessing how Qatar's curious and archaic administration systems work...if you can call it work. My residence visa was stamped into my passport in the morning, but then there was the issue of gaining an exit permit, which involved chasing the local sponsor (enigmatically named The Doctor) around town, trying to get him to sign a piece of paper giving me his permission to leave the country. Jamal, my Mr. Fix-it, told me thatwe might catch him before he left town for the weekend if we were lucky. Whatever it is that he does often involved visiting another country, or even another galaxy, battling Daleks or some other dastardly creatures. What happens if one needs to get home quickly in the case of an emergency is something I daren't dwell upon for too long.

I also had to sort out payment of the hotel bill before I could check out, and the boss from my company's Doha branch came along with me and tried to settle said bill using his credit card. The bill, being for a stay of almost four weeks, was an impressive one for over thirty thousand riyals. That's around four thousand of your English pounds. My boss had a credit card with a huge limit - more than twice that amount - but when the card was swiped, the dreaded instruction "REFER TO BANK" flashed up on the machine's screen. The boss rang the bank immediately, getting through to a human being surprisingly quickly. Then the fun started.

First of all they told him his limit wasn't as much as he believed it to be (even though it was still enough), then they told him that the maximum single transaction was ten thousand riyals, and any transactions over this amount had to be authorised following a request in writing. It was all for reasons of security, said the bank, even though they had already verified his ID with security questions at the start of the call.

The Doha boss was aghast. After an hour of phone calls to and from the bank's call centre, in addition to phone calls from the hotel management to the bank, the bank agreed to allow the transaction through if a faxed request was sent through. So the fax was sent. I had a strange feeling of inevitability about what was going to happen next, and I was right. The bank were called again to confirm that the fax had been received, but the bank said that everyone had gone home for the day, and the transaction would have to wait until Sunday. Luckily, the hotel management were sympathetic and understanding, and allowed the boss and me to leave on this basis.

This whole episode really stretched the Doha boss's patience. He is a laid back character usually, but I could see the anger building up inside him as the ordeal wore on. People in Customer Service in this part of the world are unfathomably strict in their adherence to procedure. They cannot and will not deviate from their instructions or script. Even asking for a different drink with a meal deal at McDonalds is a frustrating experience.

The final straw for the boss was getting another phone call from the bank as we headed back to the office, saying that he had given an incorrect credit card number. It turned out they had misread a hand written digit. On hanging up, the boss opened the car window and shouted an obscenity into the Doha air. I kept quiet.

When I got back to the office Mr Fix-it took me straight back out, chasing The Doctor for his prized autograph. On the way, Jamal told me that it was a good job he had a close relationship with the Doctor's driver, or things would be much harder. I just nodded and bit my tongue.

With the signature finally secured, I assumed that I would be on my way, and phoned Teresa to tell her. She cheered loudly at the news, and when Mr. Fix-it heard the cheer his face broke into a broad grin. He then told me we had to go and take the signed exit permit to the visa office near the airport to get it stamped and entered into the system. Oh, come on! Yet more red tape and yet more use of the ubiquitous *insha'allah*. What else was there to do to get out of this place? Luckily there was only a short queue at the visa office, the process was quick, and I made it to the airport in time for my flight home.

The pilot lied again. They always do. He said it was fine weather for the flight, but most of it was pretty bumpy, which was more annoying than terrifying. At last, the lights of Dubai appeared under us and we performed a sharp turn before landing nice and smoothly at DXB. We were kept on the plane for fifteen minutes or so, but then I managed to breeze through immigration and out of the airport using my e-gate card, and got home less than an hour after landing.

AS I drove along SZR towards home I was actually glad to see the familiar sights; the colourful Fairmont hotel, the white pin-prick lights on the growing Burj Dubai, and the white, billowing sail shape of the Burj Al Arab. This city is so much more vibrant than Doha; so much more alive. Oh, I know, I know. I've changed my mind *again*. What am I to do? I am confused. Some things about Dubai drive me mad, but having spent four long, lonely, boring weeks in Doha, and seeing the way the place works, I realise that I might have been hasty in dismissing the option of remaining here out of hand. It's the old greener grass thing again. The cost of living situation is still a major issue, of course, and the family definitely have to go back (unless someone has a three-bedroom villa for ninety grand going spare), but I could stay here and earn a good wage and at least not be so bored that I turn to eating and drinking excessively...although there are infinitely more opportunities to do so.

I've made the most of being home and with my loved ones, but now the weekend is almost over again, and tomorrow it's back to work in the Dubai office to face whatever music may lie in wake for me. I don't know if it's going to be a Funeral March or a Victory Serenade. There's only one way to find out.

Sunday, May 20th, 2007

The Art of Posing

Posing is big in Dubai. But there are different types of posing depending on who does it.

1. The Locals.
   The local men like nothing better than cruising up and down Dhiyafa street (linking the Sheik Zayed Road to Jumeirah Beach Road through Satwa) in their ridiculously expensive, stupidly fast, garishly flash sports cars. If you sit in one of the numerous cafés or restaurants lining said street you will see

them cruising past ever so slowly, going over the huge hump at the pedestrian lights, then turning round and coming back. They can do this for hours on end.

The local women also like to pose, but do so in shopping malls and even at work. They wander round in groups of two or three, wearing long, sequin-adorned, black *abbayas*, which leave only their faces and hands visible. They wear the largest designer sunglasses feasible and carry the most expensive handbag they can lay their hands on. They breeze about the place with an air of quiet, gracious aloofness. (Is that a word?)

2. The Western Expats.
    Western Expats like to dress up as if they are on holiday (and, yeah, it does feel like a holiday sometimes). The men wear knee-length shorts and flip-flops, the women wear summery, light dresses, and they all wear designer sunglasses either on their eyes (strangely enough) or perched atop their perfectly-coiffured heads. They then park their 4x4s along the Jumeirah Beach Road and head to the Lime Tree Café, where they order something healthy from the glowing counter staff, then lounge lazily in the comfy chairs, preferably on the terrace or balcony for (maximum pose factor), sip their soy lattés and eat some poncey bloody frittata with rocket salad or carrot cake. The carrot cake is really good, admittedly. If they haven't been able to unload them on the maid, they will sometimes bring their hideously photogenic children with them, making sure they are dressed in Osh Kosh B'Gosh or something similar, and sit them in IKEA high-chairs with a traditional wooden toy. This looks a bit strange with children over the age of seven, to be fair.

3. The Lebanese (men).
    Think heaving, darkened nightclubs with strobe lights and Richter-scale music. Think tight, white tops and copious amounts of hair gel. Enough said, really.

4. The Subcontinental Expats.
    They pose by pretending to watch everyone else pose, mostly at the public beach, or from their spluttering, dirty Nissan Sunnys as they bumble along the SZR in the middle lane at 25kmph. Those who can't afford a car pose like nodding dogs in the spluttering, dirty buses taking them to and from the

building sites. Others pose at the side of main roads, waiting for the chance to dash across between the Land Cruisers, 4x4s, Nissan Sunnies and buses. I really wish they would strike the famous clenched-fist-to-the-forehead Bruce Forsyth pose after risking death or serious injury by successfully crossing six or more lanes. I am yet to see it happen, however.

Sunday, May 27, 2007
The Heat Is On

Summer is well and truly on its way, and the opportunities to partake in outdoor pursuits are rapidly diminishing. It's still possible to sit outside in the shade at lunchtime or go for a walk on an evening, but it invariably results in sweat pooling in uncomfortable regions of the body.

But there we go: Summer is the winter of the Gulf, when the weather forces long spells inside. Everything is the wrong way round: We wear as little as is decently possible, and drink the coldest drinks available, but then for a break from the cruel, indefatigable heat, we can go to Ski Dubai and scrape our hands on the sled runs. I still have that scar from New Year's Eve.

I've been back in Dubai for over a week now, and have just about recovered my sanity after my incarceration in the twent-six-floor prison they call the Movenpick Towers hotel in Doha. No more buffets for breakfast, lunch and dinner. No more cloying attention from grinning hotel workers who pretend to worship the ground you walk on whilst secretly harbouring murderous feelings to the pampered, corpulent westerners. Instead, I actually have to make my own breakfast, load the dishwasher and wipe my own bum. It's taken some getting used to, but I think I'll manage.

The best bit of my first week back was the peace and quiet at work. The maniac scouser office manger (who has now earned the tag "Captain Chaos" amongst the senior staff) was away on holiday, and the client's people decided they had badgered me enough during my last week in Doha, so I was able to work at a leisurely pace and get on top of my work for once...instead of vice versa. Lunch hours were taken without worry, even though most of the conversation was about how bad our company was and who was going to leave next. The rest of the time I spent pondering my future, whether that is here in the Middle East, or elsewhere. Even though it was relatively quiet, the week still went quickly.

On Thursday afternoon I was invited to go for a drink by a chap called Dave, who I chat to on an internet message-board for expatriates. I have met him before through a mutual friend, so I went along to a bar called *Après* at the Mall of the Emirates where I met him and another message-board contributor called Graham, who had been giving me some stick for my musical tastes. We had a few relaxed drinks (raspberry mojitos - very, very nice) and talked about the crazy world of Dubai and the crazier world of virtual Dubai, and before I knew it, a couple of hours had disappeared, and it was time for everyone to go. It had been a nice way to round off the week, and I wouldn't mind making it a regular fixture.

And then it was the weekend again. I had been looking forward to Friday, because there was a Star Wars marathon showing all six films in sequence on one of the movie channels. We went shopping early on Friday to get it out of the way, and rushed back to the villa to get the TV on and claim our spots on the sofa. I would have missed about ten minutes of the start of Episode I, but I could live with that. The less I see of Jar Jar Binks, the better.

I didn't account for the weak link in my expectations. It turns out that I didn't have the movie channel in question in my package. I just naturally thought we would have it, but after several flicks through all two hundred plus channels of utter pap, the movie channel in question was not to be found. I was gutted, as well as annoyed with myself for assuming that paying however many hundred dirhams a month would give me the movie channels.

I rang the TV provider and asked if they could turn it on, and was told that I could, as long as I filled in thirteen different forms, took them in person to thirteen different offices, and then travelled by foot to Al Ain to milk a goat called Colin before finally getting the channel activated in forty-five working days. Forget it. The Farce is strong in this one.

JUNE

Saturday, June 02, 2007

Feeling flabby in Abu Dhabi

Emma had her third birthday on Friday, and her favourite presents seem to be the toy dishwasher and the toy medical kit she acquired. In between teeny-weeny plastic cups and plates going through the dishwasher, we were subjected to injections, stethoscope investigations and spoonfuls of invisible - but always wonderful-tasting - medicine. She had this peculiar notion that I was the one in need of the most medical attention for some reason.

After a brunch at Planet Hollywood involving balloons, fudge brownies and a nasal, American-accented rendition of Happy Birthday by a chorus of South East Asian waiting staff, we rolled home, and before long I had to depart for Abu Dhabi. Emma wasn't very happy about me going away, but I assured her my return would be swift. I had to go and see a man about an oryx, or something, and that involved an overnight stay in the UAE's capital city. So after a kiss and cuddle and another listen to my heart, I set off along Sheik Zayed road, past Jebel Ali, and out into the desert.

It wasn't long before I was almost completely alone on the highway to Abu Dhabi. The motorway looked new, with pristine white stripes and dark, even tarmac. The infinite lines of metal crash barriers separated the road from the desert, which was bleak and flat here. There wasn't much to look at, apart from the odd power line and scaffold-supported hoarding heralding yet another mega-development to swallow up the empty sand. Now and then, a lonely-looking man in traditional Pakistani dress appeared by the road, watching the traffic zip by.

Then the desert changed, and more vegetation poked through the sand on each side of the motorway, and a line of trees took up residence along the central reservation. A few settlements began to emerge, and it soon became apparent that I was in a different Emirate. The road signs changed slightly and the service stations became the blue and white-liveried Adnoc station, each with a mosque in the vicinity. One large, yellow road sign raised a chuckle, imploring the driver to BEWARE OF ROAD SURPRISES. I wonder what kind of surprises they meant; giant birthday cakes in the fast lane, or baboons on Harley Davidsons, perhaps.

Soon enough, Abu Dhabi was upon me, with the airport whizzing by on my left. I took guidance from the little map I had bought at a book shop earlier and I only went slightly wrong, approaching the city centre on a road parallel to the one I actually wanted. It was just a question of cutting across to the road I needed at some point. Abu Dhabi has a nice easy grid system of numbered roads with odd numbers running one way and even numbers the other, so there was never much danger of getting completely lost.

My inadvertent diversion was a blessing in disguise, because I managed to get a good view of the incredibly massive – and I mean *ginormous* - Zayed Grand Mosque which is still under construction. It had more shiny white domes than a convention for the follically-challenged and four tall, slender minarets that reached skywards like giant, ornate pencils. I've since heard that it has been under construction for several years now, and has been beset with problems galore. No surprises there. This is construction in the Middle East, after all.

The diversion was, as I said, a problem of miniscule proportions, and I soon found my destination. The words "hotel apartments" tend to fill me with dread these days after my experience with the accommodation I was subjected to on my arrival in Dubai last August, but I was in for a pleasant surprise. The room I was given for the night was a newly-refurbished and very pleasant apartment with separate kitchen, bedroom and lounge and even two - count them - two toilets. That's luxury to a Northerner. The kitchen was the most impressive part, with a proper cooker, a fridge freezer, a microwave, a kettle and full sets of crockery, cutlery and pans. Call me easily pleased, but I was impressed.

That night, I was entertained by a chap who works for the company I had come to meet in the morning, and we ate a perfectly adequate Mexican meal and a few tonsil-loosening beverages. After the meal, we went to a bar called Hemingway's at the Hilton hotel. It had three distinct zones within it, including a deserted night club and a lively, smoke-hazed jazz bar. The jazz bar is where we ended up, and we watched the obviously talented musicians strutting their stuff on a stage about the size of an A4 envelope. My companion for the evening told me that they used to have a grand piano on said stage, which meant the rest of the band had to huddle together in one corner. I hope they got on well.

After the jazz, which ain't really my bag, since I don't wear polo-neck sweaters and say "Nice" all the time, I was conveyed back to my hotel apartment, taking in the sights of Abu Dhabi Corniche as we went. We passed the sprawling Emirates Palace and various other landmarks on the way. There aren't as many huge skyscrapers as in Dubai, with no building over forty storeys, by my estimation. I'm sure this will change in time, as seems to be the blueprint round these parts. The amount of high buildings is obviously a barometer of a city's status and sexiness.

By daylight, AD appears to be a much greener and more tranquil place than Dubai, and yet seems livelier and more developed than Doha. I also noticed that the air is much clearer, which is a nice change when you suffer the ubiquitous dust from the construction sites that take up a pretty large slice of the land in Dubai.

AD has some construction, of course, but you get the sense that the place is far more established, with more grass and trees; almost approaching Al Ain levels in some areas. Of course if you lived here and got a bit bored with the place and had the urge to subject yourself to the in-your-face glitz and craziness of Dubai, you know it's only an hour and a bit to drive there. I don't see why you would want to do it that much, as there looks to be plenty there. It maybe doesn't attract the same headlines and events that Dubai does, but then again, AD has just won the rights to host the 2009 Formula One Grand Prix, so there must be something going for the place.

As dawn broke I had a good long lie-in and slept off the previous night's alcohol before attending my mid-morning meeting. It went well, and may well influence the decisions I need to take in terms of my next job and location.

I had made the mistake of leaving my car in an unsheltered spot overnight, without the sun shades in the front window, so by the time I jumped in it to it the temperature inside could have quite easily baked a few scones or fried a few eggs. The steering wheel was white hot and, until the AC had cooled the car down, I had to treat it like a hot potato as I navigated my way back out of AD. I stopped for a snack at an Adnoc service stop, and then continued back towards Dubai, sticking the MP3 player on shuffle mode and listening to a few banging driving tunes as the greenery of AD disappeared into the haze behind me.

You know you're approaching Dubai when you start seeing the cranes. There are new buildings shooting up at least twenty kilometres before the Ibn Battuta mall. The metro line extends right into Jebel Ali, much further than I realised, with the thick, evenly-spaced columns sprouting up all along the side of SZR up to the Trade Centre roundabout, before veering left towards the Burjuman mall and Bur Dubai. At the moment some of the columns have nothing on top, just a section of bare, rusty reinforcing steel; others have concrete plinths sat atop them which will support the u-shaped, pre-cast sections of the track bed. Quite a few more already have the track bed extending between them, the length of which increases every day. They are going at some pace, and they have to, because the metro is supposed to be working in two years' time. There weren't even any columns when I arrived ten months ago, so they are really cracking on with it.

A curious thing I've noticed about the metro is the way the raised track is designed. It doesn't go along at one level as you would expect, but rather resembles some kind of drawn-out rollercoaster ride with rises and dips taking the track over and under the many bridges and flyovers at the junctions of SZR. I'm not an engineer, but this seems a bit strange to me. I didn't think trains liked steep slopes. It will certainly be interesting to see what a train looks like going along at 100kmph as it rises and falls on this track. I hope they provide sick bags.

The whole idea of getting people to walk to the Metro stations seems a bit daft as well when you think how hot the place gets for half of the year. It will be interesting to see how, and indeed if, it works.

And then another weekend has ended, and that means work. Sunday was the day from Hell. I had been trying to meet several deadlines at the end of last week, and with three major ones on my shoulders jockeying for priority, I had to try and manage my time in an effective manner. I sometimes struggle to do this, especially with the impossible deadlines and demands that Middle Eastern companies seem to have, and managed to meet the sum total of none of my major deadlines. I was too tired to work the weekend, and I had prior commitments anyway, so the mess I had to clear up on Sunday was not good. I had snotty e-mails from client, lectures from managers and phone calls from crazed engineers, all telling me I was crap and making me feel crapper. By the end of the day I had put out most of the fires that had flared up, but it was bloody hard work. What I need now is a long holiday, just two weeks of doing nothing. I'm scheduled to go back to the UK for two weeks mid-July, and I can't wait.

Monday, June 25, 2007
Fun and games in the sand pit.

Yes, I'm still here. I've had a curious couple of weeks, and am just itching to get back to the UK for a good break from this place. I paid a little visit there the other weekend, to attend to some personal business (more options for the future, possibly) and also took the chance to visit my parents and brother in North Yorkshire. This involved leaving Dubai on Thursday night on the overnight flight, landing in London on Friday morning, attending to my business, taking the train to York, arriving at about 4pm, wishing I had brought a jacket (it was wet and very cold), going for dinner with the family, going to sleep for a long time, waking up to a full English breakfast, going for lunch in a nice café, then catching the train back to London to catch the plane back to the sand pit, managing to catch less than an hour of shut-eye on the cramped, noisy Emirates flight that took off ninety minutes late....phew.

This would have been bad enough, but as it was, my journey was not finished. I collected my suitcase and checked in for the flight to Doha for a working-week-long visit. Oh joy. I managed to get through Sunday on adrenaline alone, and after nodding off at my desk a few times, decided to go to the hotel (a flea-pit called the Regency, no more high-end places for me) and sleep. I slept like a baby, but without the crying and soiling.

The week went OK, and quite quickly, but by the end of it, my tiredness levels weren't much improved and I felt that I was on the verge of my first proper AF attack since last November. It doesn't help that I have put most of the weight that I lost back on, or that I have been drinking and eating far too much for my own good. The old craw and stomach have been complaining for a while, and greet most types of alcoholic intake with sharp, painful protest. Do I listen? What do you think?

So there I am, Wednesday night, finding myself lying on my bed watching the classic '80s film, *Ferris Bueller's Day Off.* The mini-bar sits there, silently tempting me with its chocolate and Tuc biscuits and fizzy drinks. Having eaten a very presentable curry at one of the few eateries in Doha I actually like (an Indian restaurant near the Tennis stadium), I should have been sated. But no, I just had to have the Toblerone, and gave in. And lo and behold, as Ferris' day came to an end, my oesophagus lurched and my heart did a little flip, and I was in AF.

Oh, for fuck's sake. Not here...not now!

I was annoyed and scared. I didn't know where I could go or who I could call, so decided to try and sleep it off: a tactic that has worked before. I really did not want to go to hospital, especially as I was booked on the 3pm flight back to Dubai the next day.

It didn't work. I woke up with my heart still jittering around unevenly, so I rang the Dubai office and they told me I would have to pay for treatment myself and claim it back. Fair enough. I then rang my colleagues in Doha and arranged for a lift to the hospital. It was more of a clinic, actually, and the chap taking me there had enormous trouble finding it. It's a good job I wasn't actually dying.

After an hour of sitting and sighing in the waiting area, I finally saw the doctor and he immediately told me to go to another, bigger hospital. I was taken in an ambulance, which was good fun. They had the full blues and twos thing going on, and the journey was quite quick. The Land Cruiser drivers must have been feeling generous today and let me through.

And so the usual routine started, and they jabbed me with IV needles and stuck ECG leads all over me. The first nurse was impatiently rough with me. It was a government hospital and was very busy, especially in the emergency room. Various men in various states were wheeled in looking forlorn and moaning and crying from their injuries. A few women in full veils came in as well. They probably would've looked forlorn as well, if their faces had been visible. Even when in pain and suffering, these women still feel the need to maintain their modesty to the outside world.

Eventually I was admitted to the coronary care unit, and placed in a ward with three other men. No private rooms in this place, matey. My companions included a Filipino, and Indian and an old Arab man. The Arab was almost constantly surrounded by visitors, the Filipino spent all his time on his mobile phone and the Indian seemed to have a compulsive disorder that involved ringing the speaking clock on speaker-phone. He even did this in the middle of the night, when he wasn't snoring loudly and explosively. This marvellous noise was interspersed with the Arab chap shouting for Allah or arguing with nurses carrying needles. When I did manage to sleep, the nurses woke me up to stick more needles in me, either to draw blood or inject drugs. They have to do this on a regular basis to check for heart enzymes or something.

I was fully expecting to be zapped with the defibrillator again, like I was in November. I was praying for them to just get on with it, but they persevered with the IV drugs route and, by Jove (or Allah or whatever deity was on duty), it worked. At about 4pm on the day I was admitted, my heart sneakily reverted to blissful normal sinus rhythm. I called the male nurse to tell him and he doubted it, but I reminded him that I was an expert, having had the condition for seven years. I knew when I was in AF, and I knew when it was in NSR. So he did another ECG and confirmed it. Super.

I thought I might get home that day, but the doctors insisted that I wait to see the consultant the following morning. I thought it over and decided that it would probably be the best course of action. If I took the option of going home, it would have involved a flight and all that rushing about and walking round airports. The rest would do me good, I thought, forgetting about my noisy companions.

I shouldn't forget to mention the Doha Mr. Fix-it, Jamal. He came to see me at the hospital and made sure I had everything I needed. He brought me biscuits and mobile phone batteries and was generally a really good help, especially in the absence of a family to visit me. After the consultant had seen and discharged me on Friday morning, he picked me up and conveyed me to the airport to catch the 1pm flight back to Doha. His weekend attire was a complete change from his working week clothing; he was wearing a brilliant white dish-dash and skull-cap. I didn't recognise him at first when he entered the ward. For his generous help and care - well beyond the call of duty - I am eternally grateful.

So on to the plane I got, and the pilot told us it was going to be bumpy. It wasn't at all until we were on final approach to Dubai, and then it was just a bit turbulent with a strong cross-wind giving our pilots a good work-out. I think these pilots mess with our emotions. When they say conditions are good, it is invariably a bumpy ride and vice-versa. I finally got home after my globe-trotting and back into the arms of my family. They were pleased to see me but bitterly disappointed that the bags of Jelly Babies I had brought back from the UK were now just amorphous blobs of coloured jelly. My suitcase had obviously been sat in the sunshine at the airport for some time.

And now I'm waiting for the nebulous future to form. I need a holiday. I need to give my body a break from the heat and the poor nutrition. I've decided to stop drinking alcohol full-stop, which can only be a good thing, even if I get questioning looks at social gatherings. I need to get back on track and back into the right frame of mind to sort my health problems out. I am sick of being sick, as I think I might have mentioned before, but I need to sort out a few other issues first, like my future. All I know is that it lies somewhere other than Dubai.

JULY

Sunday, July 01, 2007

They're Gone!

Ten months after they arrived, they have left Dubai and gone back to North Yorkshire. And I feel sorry for myself; more sorry than usual.

It finally happened, and now the whole thing feels like a strange dream. My darling wife and children got on the plane to Manchester last night. I was able to stay with them through the check-in and helped them through a horrendous check-in queue and an unexpected over-weight luggage trauma. I had to take six kilos of stuff back home with me to avoid the excessive excess baggage fees. I said goodbye to my family just before passport control, and my little girl started crying as I bent down to kiss her on the head.

We all had a good blub in the end. Joseph had a cry during our last ever meal as a family in Dubai, Teresa suffered from leaky eyes a couple of nights ago and I was set off by a song on the radio on the way to the airport. Even Joseph's teacher had a cry on his last day at school.

It's not like anyone's died or anything, and this separation is only for a couple of weeks, but it's like I said before: goodbyes are painful. It seems to get harder every time. I think what has made it even worse this time is coming back from the airport to the half-empty villa with its echoing walls. I lay awake for a long time last night, feeling like I was in a strange bed in someone else's house. The lack of a night light shining through the gap in the door from the passage made me feel on edge.

Coming back from work today was difficult and emotion-laden as well, although work isn't much fun now that I've told them I'm leaving the company. They have taken it badly, almost personally, but I think the fact that I am only one of four departures amongst senior staff isn't helping matters. Maybe they should ponder the reasons for this. Maybe I would have stuck it out another year out if things had been different. Maybe.

So I drove up to the villa, parked the car and opened the door. Instead of children running to hug me, I was greeted by no sound other than the echo of my shuffling footsteps on the tiles. The lack of a TV to just turn on and fill the void doesn't help either. We sold most of the furniture and appliances at a yard sale a few weeks ago, opening our house to a flock of vultures that came and picked away at the bones of our Dubai life, taking away what gave it any feeling of homeliness. All the things that we couldn't sell act as reminders of my solitude, sinking their little sharp teeth into me; a bag of unused toy bricks here; small, empty beds there. And now the departure of Teresa and the kids has left it as a shell. I don't think of it as home anymore.

Luckily, I don't have to stay in this villa long. I've been assigned a house to look after for someone who is away, and I move in at the weekend. They have a telly at least, and there are no memories there; not my memories anyway.

I don't know why I feel so utterly saddened and frankly pissed off about it. I think I'm sad because I feel like I've failed. We decided that we can't stay here as a family and make any money, which is primarily why we came, and I can't help thinking that we should have tried a bit longer. I failed to do enough research into costs, and I naively believed the hype fed to my by employment agencies and by my company. The family enjoyed it here, for all its faults. Joseph had a fantastic year at his school, winning an Achievement Award and scoring really well in his SATs. I worry that he won't get the same standard of education back in the UK.

But then I remember when I tentatively, half-jokingly suggested the return to the UK back in April just after my parents had gone home. My wife and my son were so excited at the idea. I know where their hearts lie, but I just hope this taste of another life has given them the appetite for further adventures in the future. Maybe when things are a bit more settled and secure.

Maybe when I get on top of my health problems.

Maybe when hell freezes over, eh? Always the optimist.

Like I say, it's been an experience for us all, and life is about experiences. Or is it about vainly trying to delay the inevitable? Or maybe it's about experiencing as much as you can before the inevitable...Oh, please shut up.

Dubai has been an eye-opener, there is no argument there. It wasn't what I expected at all. I never expected the wafer-thin facade to slip away so quickly, revealing not just clashes of cultures, but a conflicting torment at the heart of a city that is trying to be all things to all people. I didn't expect it to dawn on me that behind the malls and hotels and beaches there really isn't much here.

The shallowness of the place and the people, especially the western expats, has really surprised me. I never expected to get so infuriated and frustrated at the bare-faced hubris and casual carelessness of the driving. I never expected the completely shameless incompetence of the customer "service" provision or the obstinate ignorance of the general public when they wrap themselves in their little, safe bubbles.

I failed to anticipate how bad the four to five months of intense heat would be, with humidity that bears down on you with the density of treacle, rendering even breathing a labour-intensive task. I never expected to see fleets of aging white buses ferrying sad, hollowed-out men from their disgusting labour camps to the building sites and back. I had no idea that the colonial-style pecking order would be so utterly enshrined in the way of life here. The Arabian Gulf keeps a discreet veil over the metaphorical but huge gulf that exists between the haves and have-nots.

I never expected my feelings to be so mixed, because on the flip-side there is a lifestyle of luxury and privilege available if you have the right money and the right background...and as long as you keep those gold-tinted sunglasses on.

I have battled with my thought over my decision to leave, but a good friend asked me a question before I moved here, and now I can see where he's coming from.

He asked, "Who are they building it all for? Who is going to live there?"

I couldn't answer him then, and I can't answer him now.

From a small desert settlement centred round the creek, this metropolis has materialised like a mirage from the barren sands of the Arabian Desert. In the space of forty years - less time than I have been alive – this city has flourished in the most inhospitable of places, and it has only just started, if the rulers have their way. The scale of the construction taking place or proposed to take place is truly staggering, but I get the sense that the infrastructure is being added or altered as an after-thought.

I just don't understand how it can be sustainable. The power and water requirements for what is already here are staggering; the UAE is one of if not *the* biggest consumers of resources per capita in the world. It just doesn't ring true. The powers-that-be have amazing visions of vast cities full of vibrant culture and a lifestyle to aspire to, but I wonder if they've ever heard the saying, "In dreams begin responsibilities."

I really hope it doesn't all fall down round their ears, but I just sense that the place doesn't have enough backbone, enough foundation to keep going the way it is. It is all built on sand, after all.

I'm leaving Dubai shortly, and this has been a place for me to vent my feelings and record my life here. It was all my own opinions from my own perspective. I hope it has informed and entertained those of you who have stumbled across it.

Bye for now.

Christopher R. Combe.

August 2006 – July 2007

Printed in Great Britain
by Amazon.co.uk, Ltd.,
Marston Gate.